FOLDED
WISDOM

FOLDED WISDOM

Notes from Dad on Life, Love, and Growing Up

JOANNA GUEST

CELADON
BOOKS
NEW YORK

FOLDED WISDOM. Copyright © 2019 by Joanna Guest.
Illustrations copyright © 2019 by Robert Guest.
All rights reserved. Printed in the United States of America.
For information, address Celadon Books, 175 Fifth Avenue,
New York, N.Y. 10010.

www.celadonbooks.com

The notes on pages 22, 25, 33, 143, 145, 147, 165, and 183
previously appeared in *Esopus Magazine*, Spring 2009.

Photographs by Tamara Staples
Cover design by Anne Twomey
Designed by Steven Seighman

ISBN 978-1-250-20779-1 (paper over board)
ISBN 978-1-250-20778-4 (ebook)

Our books may be purchased in bulk for promotional,
educational, or business use. Please contact your local
bookseller or the Macmillan Corporate and Premium Sales
Department at 1-800-221-7945, extension 5442, or by email
at MacmillanSpecialMarkets@macmillan.com.

First Edition: May 2019

10 9 8 7 6 5 4 3 2 1

To Bob, Gloria, and Theo

the beginning

MY DAD IS what you'd call a "morning person"—he feels he is his best self at the crack of dawn. He is also a creature of habit. These days, he wakes up at five A.M. and heads to Prospect Park near our home in Brooklyn. He alternates his weekdays between going there with our dog or with his bike—both of which he loves and both of which have him covering somewhere between five and nineteen miles before the workday begins.

When I was growing up, he also followed a morning routine, but that one was a bit different. Every morning he would wake up before the rest of us, take the dog out for a walk (at the time we had Sunny; now his four-legged friend is Bear), then return home to get settled at the kitchen table. There he'd sit, with a cup of coffee and a lit candle or two, open up a six-by-nine pad of plain white paper, and write.

What he wrote varied over the years—but the routine and recipients never shifted: beginning in 1995 and continuing for the next fourteen years until we each graduated from high school, he would settle in every school morning and write both my younger brother, Theo, and me a note. He would take a moment, alone with his thoughts before the day became hectic, to reflect; he wrote and drew and put a piece of himself on paper for us to carry into the day, every day.

My rough estimates say this means he wrote us 4,775 notes. Today, we still have more than 3,500 of them.

The notes began as illustrations, accompanied by a few words, and were tucked into lunchboxes alongside our sandwiches. As we got older, more and more sentences filled the page, and the little pieces of paper were folded up into triangles, like paper footballs, waiting on the kitchen counter to be grabbed on our way out the door.

The daily missives evolved alongside us—filled with thoughts that were sometimes personal and other times universal. Sometimes they'd congratulate us on a good test score, or an impressive strikeout; they'd reflect on an argument, an incident of sibling rivalry; they'd be about friendships and love, and also about differences and disappointment; they'd teach a lesson, or apologize for setting a bad example; they'd often remark on the weather, or words would be strung together in rhyme; they might reflect on an untimely passing, and at other times on a life well lived; sometimes they'd capture history— of what was happening within our family and on the front page of the newspaper.

Many of us have a morning routine. And occasionally those routines get shaken up because life happens—we get sick; we sleep through the alarm; an unexpected work trip pops up; we feel down, uninspired. This, of course, happened to my dad, too, but somehow it never disrupted the opportunity and genuine commitment he felt toward sharing himself with us.

Sitting down late at the kitchen table might mean his note was brief or didn't include color illustrations. And a week of traveling meant he wracked his brain to write out a series of notes ahead of time, explaining why he had to be out of town (*There are so many times in life when you have to do things you don't like. This is one of them for me. I don't mind the work, but I hate being away. At night is the worst . . . I hope you are sleeping with Mom so she doesn't have to be alone*), telling us he missed us (*Thank you for your patience, honey. I know you miss me a lot. I know I miss you a lot too*), and, always, sending his love alongside the promise he'd be home soon (*Home again! I'm comin' home again! To stay longer would be a sin! I can't wait to get home to the family din! Hug you and grab you and give you a spin! Kiss you and kiss you again and again! Have fun today—work hard and then . . . I'll be home again!*).

At a certain point, this routine became more than a preferred way to start the day—it was the only way.

You have no idea how peaceful it is to sit at the kitchen table with a candle or two burning and a cup of coffee in front of you and a pen in hand ready to write. I love getting up ahead of everyone and having that hour to myself and my thoughts. It's a very helpful, meditative way to start the day. It gives me a chance to think about myself, about you and Theo and Mom. And writing to you gives me another chance. A chance to connect with you—share my thoughts—my life with you. A chance to give you something of my private self. Without feedback of any kind, which is a plus and a minus but hey—that's life.

Note to Joanna, January 23, 2002 (age 13, 8th grade)

Hey ♥ Joanna Ruth -
Wednesday
January 23, 2002

You have no idea how peaceful it is to sit at the kitchen table with a candle or two burning and a cup of coffee in front of you and a pen in hand ready to write. I love getting up ahead of everyone and having that hour to myself and my thoughts. It's very helpful, meditative way to start the day. It gives me a chance to think about myself, about you and Theo and mom. And writing to you gives me another chance. A chance to connect with you - share my thoughts - my life with you. A chance to give you something of my private self. Without feedback of any kind which is a plus and a minus but hey - That's life. I love you.

Dad

I now understand that my dad's dedication to this form of morning meditation and reflection evolved naturally out of the particulars of his own childhood and early adult life.

Robert (everyone calls him "Bob," and often I do, too) is the fourth of eight children—five boys, three girls. His father, Rear Admiral Frank Guest, was out to sea with the U.S. Navy for most of his upbringing, and his ever-patient mother, Joan, spent her days trying to control their growing herd of children. They moved thirteen times during his childhood. He attended eight schools in seven cities between first and twelfth grade. Naturally, his best friends were his siblings—it was hard to maintain the fleeting outside friendships that were made in each new town. He felt his personal relationship with his own father, however, was minimal—one-on-one time was rare, owing to competition among siblings and my grandfather's military duties. While he never says a bad word about his upbringing, my dad remembers having all of one conversation alone with his father in their short time together. I never had the chance to meet my grandfather; he passed away when my dad was only twenty-three.

My parents met in 1976 at Pratt Institute in Brooklyn. Bob was a sculpture major and my mom, Gloria, was in the industrial design program. They met in drawing class, and my dad was in love within ten days. (I say this with confidence because I recently found a letter he wrote to his friend Brian in which he declares, in no uncertain terms, this love: *Gloria and I have only known each other 10 days and it seems like all my life and at the same time not at all . . . I love Gloria, Brian. I don't need to read it in a book by Kant or in a poem by Whitman. I do. I love her.* Turns out he's always had a way with words.)

After graduating, Gloria went to work for a design firm in New York City while Bob supported his large public art installations with random side jobs (at one point opening a company called Snappy Construction–"If You're Going to Make It, Make It Snappy"). In 1986, after ten years of dating, they decided to formally settle down and were married in a small chapel at their alma mater. That same year they incorporated their new exhibit production business, which continues until this day.

By the fall of 1995, my parents were nearing the ten-year marker in their business and marriage, and they now had my brother and me—a four- and seven-year-old. It was this fall that the daily notes began.

Years later I asked my dad what sparked his interest and kept him inspired to write to us every day. The commitment seemed daunting and perhaps unrealistic (to me and nearly anyone I mention it to). The spark had initially come from the prompting of Theo's preschool teacher, he told me. It was a simple suggestion, something like: "We want to encourage Theo's interest in reading. If you wrote him something small to bring to school, that might provide the extra push he needs to practice." This prompt was all it took. From that moment on, he became dedicated to writing to each of us, and the notes felt only natural to him for three reasons:

For starters, in the midst of competing demands to be a good dad, husband, and businessman, he felt the days becoming predictable and full: wake up, walk the dog, and say a quick "have a good day" before we were all hurrying out the door. Then, upon returning home, everyone was exhausted from our respective days at work and school. We would catch up with each other, but it often felt obligatory and peripheral to him. He wanted to find a way to share himself—his thoughts, humor, frustration, and love—at the time of day when he felt his best. He realized that if he could create a brief pause in the morning, he could use the time to write and reveal those parts of himself that weren't coming through after a long day's work.

Secondly, as an artist, he was frustrated. He had gone years since graduating from Pratt without fully dedicating himself to his artwork. Writing and illustrating the notes became a small way to exercise his creative muscle. He was happy with a pen in hand, and had been ever since his early twenties when he discovered his passion for art and began carrying sketchbooks on him at all times. The notes evolved out of this comforting habit of pondering on the page. The only difference was that now there was an intended audience to absorb his creativity and writing.

Finally, he wanted to build a stronger connection with Theo and me than he had with his own father. He felt like he struggled with oral communication (*I've never been very good at conversation, have you noticed?*), and as someone brimming with thoughts and feelings, he was eager to explore what he could, and how he might, share with his own kids—What did we react best to? What was too much? What was not enough? All he knew was that he did not want to be walled off from us the way he often felt his own father was, and he wanted to use his words to let us know who he was as both a person and as our dad.

Bob, Gloria, Joanna, Theo, and their dog, Sunny,
in Mount Desert Island, Maine.
Hand-colored family holiday card, 1998.

Over the years, we would return home with the notes crumpled up in lunchboxes, backpacks, and back pockets, and—somehow—my mom, always one to save English papers, physics review sheets, and art projects, would take our notes and put them aside in drawers and shoeboxes. She never read them—unless she found one mostly disintegrated from a trip through the washing machine. "They weren't addressed to me," she says.

I remember that as I began to apply to college, one of my teachers suggested I write the personal statement about my dad's notes. I shot down the idea—and my rosacea came on full display as another adult acknowledged this detail about my family. What on earth would I say about that? I wondered.

I also knew that my friends had a growing interest in seeing what was inside—sometimes asking if they could sit with me as I unfolded the paper (to them, perhaps this was something special already). I didn't think much about where the notes would go once they were read, but I didn't want to lose one; I felt horrible when one took a trip through the wash because it wasn't taken out of my jeans, and I can still remember just how guilty I felt if the hours slipped away and I made it home without ever opening the note to see what he'd written. I remember trying to quickly unfold the triangle before anyone else found out what I'd done—as if someone were watching—wrinkling the page a bit to make sure it appeared read and clearly unfolded.

And while the opportunity to write my college essay on these notes has long since passed, maybe it was for the best. It was hard to see and understand the value of their messages while standing so close to them, so inside of this experience that was my own version of ordinary. Just as my dad had a ritual of writing, I had one of reading. I expected the notes to be there, and that expectation was never left unmet.

Now, ten years after the last note was penned to Theo in 2009, I've unfolded and read through all 3,514 that remain.

In many ways, I've experienced the notes in an entirely new way at this age and found lessons that ring even truer today than they did when I was, let's say, thirteen. Viewing the notes together, side by side with so many others, has left me amazed, enamored, and inspired by what was always there, tucked inside those little pieces of paper, just waiting to be reabsorbed.

But the idea of the notes being revisited was never something my dad intended. They were a gift of the moment, a rumination on the day ahead, a lesson to touch and think about in whatever way we could at whatever age we were, and then move on from, knowing that there were more to come. While we had an expectation to receive them, my dad never had an expectation that they would return home. Yet return home so many did. My mom saved them without fanfare or acknowledgment, believing that one day we might want to learn from and cherish what was written on the page. And I had to be older to appreciate more completely their deeper value.

Collectively our notes are filled with "simple beauty"—they are unvarnished, raw, human expressions that display my dad's never-ending attempt to make sure we didn't take any daily beauty for granted.

The routine was uniquely suited for my dad in many ways, but what he wrote wasn't always uniquely suited for only Theo and me. Often, the notes were filled with lessons and thoughts that we could all use to consider and digest—about how we treat successes and failures, communicate frustration and praise, express happiness, sadness, and love to one another, and experience the world around us. And so while this story itself is a public homage to my dad—and a thank-you to him for this gift—it also serves as a reminder to everyone working on relationships in their own lives: we're not always perfect and wise communicators, and we all differ in the chosen method for expressing ourselves, but there is great value—and greater reward—in consistently grappling with and revealing who we are to one another.

In the morning sometimes I'm struck by the simple beauty that we take for granted every day. If only we would open our eyes—tune our brains to the wondrous beauty channel and see the amazing things that are right before our eyes.

A morning picture for you. Enjoy!

Note to Joanna, March 7, 2002 (age 13, 8th grade)

Hey ♡ Joanna Roth.

Thursday
March 7, 2002

In the morning sometimes
I'm struck by the simple
beauty that we take for
granted every day. If
only we would open our
eyes - tune our brains to
the wonderous beauty
channel and see
the amazing
things that
are right
before
our eyes.

A morning picture
for you.
Enjoy!
Love
Dad

Visual notes from preschool
through the fourth grade

MUCH OF THE INITIAL drive toward writing the notes stemmed from my dad's desire to express himself creatively. As a student at Pratt, he filled his portfolio with large-scale projects—often pushing the boundaries of traditional sculpture work and seeking new ways for viewers to interact with and experience art. One such project was a proposal to hang clotheslines between the World Trade towers in New York. He sketched this idea out over multiple years, envisioning how he would engineer the lines and keep the clothes secure in the wind. Finally, to complete the proposal, he used a classic Butterick pattern and sewed together a thirty-foot-tall short-sleeved red shirt with twelve-inch-diameter buttons to scale. Then, in the middle of the night before graduation day in 1979, he, my mom, and some friends climbed to the roof of two dormitory buildings at the center of campus and hung the giant garment from a steel cable stretched between them.

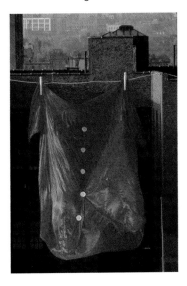

The Big Red Shirt, Pratt Institute, 1979.

While Pratt's campus was as far as the laundry would make it, the effort was so notable that the school mistakenly granted him a second degree in fashion design (true story!). Shortly after the Big Red Shirt surprised students, teachers, and administrators alike, my dad was interviewed for the school newspaper. After being asked where the idea for this project came from, he replied: "This big idea came out of my little head!"

It wouldn't surprise me if he summed up his dedication to writing our daily notes in much the same way.

The notes he wrote us were far smaller in size than the artwork of his past, and they didn't become a large collection until many years had elapsed. And while we may not have understood what was coming out of his "little head" as extraordinary in the moment, today, with the benefit of hindsight, it feels like the notes have become something of a "big idea."

In a sketchbook from college, my dad writes:

What is art to me except a lot of silliness.
At least a lot of times it comes out that way.

During our younger years, the notes were filled with illustrations. Bob's love of drawing meant we'd unfold these pages during lunchtime to discover magical flowers, superheroes, and sketches of our favorite dinosaurs and baseball players.

Filling the notes with illustrations was a helpful and "silly" way to grab the attention of young kids, but he enjoyed treating the page as a blank canvas for a larger purpose. Each sheet presented him with the opportunity to show us his creative and curious side—a side we knew about from the imaginative art of his that was hanging around our house, and the over-the-top Halloween costumes he and our mom sewed for us every year, but it was not something we understood as an integral part of his identity just yet.

He expressed his feelings and explored his mind by drawing and writing in sketchbooks all throughout his early adult years, and so later, as a parent, he began to touch on and dissect the new feelings that came with that role and responsibility using the same old tools.

Note to Theo, November 2, 1995 (age 4, preschool)

Throughout the notes, we visually learned about our dad's mind and personality as we read through the colorful messages filled with his signature optimism and creativity.

The notes began like this because that is what we could handle—we were young kids. Theo was still learning how to read when the notes started making their way into his lunchbox, and we were both understanding more and more every day how to think critically and use our own imagination.

Note to Theo, November 10, 1995 (age 4, preschool)

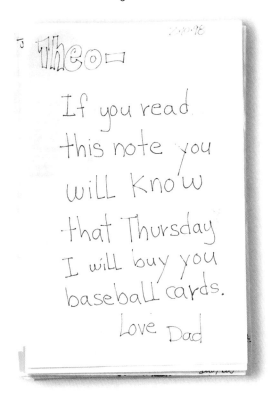

Note to Theo, February 10, 1998 (age 6, 1st grade)

The notes from our younger years were experimental. Which questions did we respond to? If he asked us to answer a math problem, or to circle a series of spelling words, did we do it? If he asked us to think about a particular issue facing us, did it seem like we gave it some thought? He used the notes to figure out the answers to these questions, constantly coming up with new ways to deliver his love, enthusiasm, and guidance.

Note to Joanna, September 15, 1995
(age 7, 2nd grade)

Note to Theo, May 13, 1997
(age 5, kindergarten)

The colorful communication we received every day from preschool through the fourth grade taught us little lessons, gave us something to look at and think of our dad, and, ultimately, met us where we were: being kids.

Note to Theo, April 9, 1999 (age 7, 2nd grade)

Note to Theo, November 13, 1995 (age 4, preschool)

¡ Joanna   9·12·95

Hats on your head.
Hats on a rack.
Hats hiding in your pack.

Hats on your knee
   in church.
Hats that you find
   after a search.

Hats that blow off
   your head in a storm.
Hats (when it's cold)
Keep you snug, dry
   and warm.
Hats that tell us
   who you are.
Hats that help us
   see real far.
Hats are cool!   Dad/Bob

Note to Joanna, September 12, 1995 (age 7, 2nd grade)

Note to Joanna, February 8, 1996 (age 7, 2nd grade)

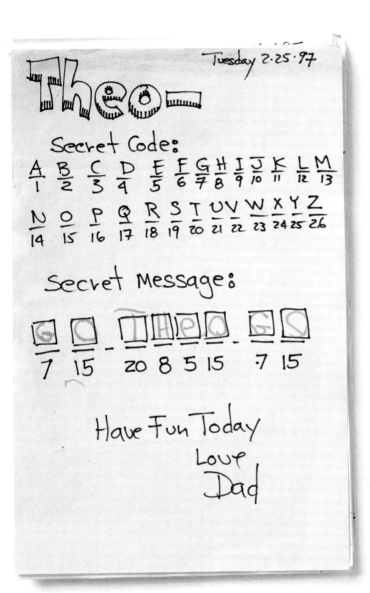

Note to Theo, February 25, 1997 (age 5, kindergarten)

Best Job in the World

Notes about parenting, feeling proud,
and growing up together

ONE OF THE THINGS my dad says he loves about being a dad is that he has two kids, and two kids only—one girl and one boy. He has an abundance of love, and it is perfectly shared between the two of us, without strain or fear of favoritism.

This specific appreciation for having a literal "couple" of kids likely stems from the fact that his own parents had eight children, with a new baby arriving every two to three years—Marcia, Frank, Rick, Bob, Jim, Ellen, Steve, and Joni. It's hard, maybe impossible, to provide individual attention to so many kids.

When my dad talks about his life today, he considers himself a father first and foremost. Everything else comes after that. He is then a husband. Then a friend. And finally, a business owner. But mostly, he's a dad. It is the most important job he has.

Being a dad is not easy sometimes, but I tell you . . . It's the best job in the world!! Just because we get upset now and then or we don't always see eye-to-eye doesn't mean we don't love each other. We love each other very much.

Note to Joanna, November 10, 1997 (age 9, 4th grade)

I'm your dad! And my job is to do whatever I can for you, Joanna, and your mom. Sometimes I get to do what I want that's just for me—but most of the time taking care of my family is what I want to do.

Note to Theo, June 6, 2002 (age 10, 5th grade)

Any job we approach and take on as humans involves a learning curve. Right off the bat, there's excitement and anxiety as we learn the tricks of the trade; we experiment, fail, and succeed, again and again. This process is essential, and the acknowledgment that we aren't perfect from the start invites reflection as we figure out what works best, which tools and skills we need to fine-tune, and how best to juggle new responsibilities with past priorities. For my dad, the job of parenting was no exception; he was learning every day, experimenting, succeeding, and failing, and his reflections on those experiences were often explored within our notes.

As kids, we rarely measure our performance on the job of being daughters and sons. We don't grade ourselves on how we make our parents feel, how we communicate what we want, or what we could do to make their lives easier. For most of growing up, our parents and guardians are the people we need to survive, and so we think more about what we can get from them and less about how we can give in return.

Illustration from Bob's sketchbook, 1994

Many days, my dad would suggest we reflect on the thoughts he was presenting about his own efforts and then decide if we could help him be better by doing something on our end. He asked us to consider our own role within the family unit—and reminded us that we, too, had unique jobs as children. In an effort to be the best he could be at the job he valued the most, he wanted to make sure we understood that we were on this journey together.

Every day I try to be the kind of guy
worthy to be called "Dad."
And when I sometimes fail, I stumble and flail,
you know I'm feeling sad.
We're only human—you and me.
With all our problems there to see.
So no use getting mad.
I'll try to understand you, and if you try too,
we'll both be really glad.

Note to Joanna, January 13, 1998 (age 9, 4th grade)

Trust is so important Theo. You need to trust me and I need to trust you. When I tell you I will do something, I make every effort to do it. When I ask you to do something, I expect you to do it as well.

Note to Theo, March 27, 2003 (age 11, 6th grade)

There was also a sense of wonder within the notes that focused on the role of parenting and what it meant for him to raise good, independent, and compassionate children. Whether he was illustrating the highlights of fatherhood like reading together, or writing about the range of emotions he experienced as he watched us grow, there are many notes that focus on how he felt being in the front row during this phase of never-ending discovery.

I love you for your drive, your determination, your energy and enthusiasm, your desire for balance, the way you're in touch with the deep flowing currents of your feelings. You have more talents than you know. Live and discover them!

Note to Joanna, September 28, 2005 (age 17, 12th grade)

The notes were intended to meet us at a particular age. But over the many years, one recurring theme was a reminder to embrace the age we were currently in and appreciate the process of growing up. He wanted us to understand that it takes time to become an adult. Life moves fast, and while it might seem exciting to be older and wiser already, it'll be here before you know it, so enjoy the moment.

You are 11½ years old and you've tried a lot of things. Have you tried everything? There is so much more waiting for you in your life. Waiting for you to discover—mountains to climb! Oceans to sail! Deserts to cross! Some challenges you will win. Sometimes you will lose. Play to win and never give up. Be proud of yourself always!

Note to Theo, February 27, 2003 (age 11, 6th grade)

There's a whole life out there waiting to live one day, one month, one year at a time. It's zoomin' by so fast. Take your time. Feel what's going on with you, with your friends, with your family . . . Mom and I can point at opportunities, choices, ideas, but you look into them or not. You're twelve, not twenty one, but you will be one day, so live now, now . . . Have fun. Be twelve. Look ahead. Take your time. Think! Feel! Grow!

Note to Joanna, March 13, 2001 (age 12, 7th grade)

While I don't know how it feels to be a parent, I do think I know how it feels to build, support, and take care of the relationships I have with those closest to me. There are many different advice columns and guidebooks out there with tips on growing up and how to be the best friend, partner, sibling, or parent you can be. It seems one constant piece of advice reiterated within the notes is agreed upon as true—we all must seek to understand ourselves. You learn as you go; you learn from times when you make mistakes, when you say the right thing, say the wrong thing, or say nothing at all. We all grow and change, and over time, try to balance who we are, what we want, and how we can be our best self, with others by our side.

> You are really growing up—becoming more responsible—and it's a pleasure to see . . . It's not easy, I know. In fact, it's really hard to mature. Lots of people never make it—never grow up, and stay kids in big bodies. What is "grown up"? What does it mean to become one? I guess you ask that question to ten different people and you'll get ten different answers. To me? Well I guess it means being able to find balance between satisfying my own needs and the needs of others. Of understanding between my needs and wants in the first place. And that's just the tip of the iceberg as they say!
>
> Note to Joanna, January 18, 2001 (age 12, 7th grade)

As I read the notes now, it becomes clear that they not only chronicle the growth of Theo and me—but my dad as well.

The road to maturity we walk on all of our lives. It's a joy to walk it with you!

Note to Theo, March 11, 2005 (age 13, 8th grade)

June '88 I became a father, what an indescribable joy—the beginning of a new life. What lies ahead? Who will she become? What will she be like? Will I be a good father to her? A good husband? Life got very full, very complicated, very beautiful, filled with love that June. Now it's June '03. A new century. A different time for sure. A lot has happened. A lot left to go. The same questions seek answers—What lies ahead? Who will she become? Am I a good father and husband? We know more about ourselves 15 years later yet we still don't know the whole story. It's still being written. And it will continue to be written until and beyond the days we die. All we can do is love—love the best way we can.

Note to Joanna, June 2, 2003 (age 14, 9th grade)

His evolution from father of little kids to father of middle schoolers to father of high schoolers is written out on the page—day after day, year after year. And the evolution of that role—to this day—is what he considers to be the best job in the world.

When you have a child your life is forever changed, forever enriched, forever filled with joy and pain—a delicious joy and pain. They go hand in hand and it's way better to accept and embrace both than to never have either at all.

Note to Theo, March 13, 2008 (age 16, 11th grade)

Note to Theo, October 21, 1999 (age 8, 3rd grade)

Note to Theo, October 22, 1999 (age 8, 3rd grade)

Note to Joanna, October 4, 2002 (age 14, 9th grade)

There's many things that hurt, that sting our bodies and our feelings. Some parents nudge—try to mold our lives, like kneading fudge into a mold. Is the shape they try to make right for you? Or is it fake? I was a kid, I'm a father now, trying to do his best somehow. With Mom, with Theo, with you. Holy cow!

Note to Joanna, March 31, 2000 (age 11, 6th grade)

Hey Joanna Ruth

Friday
03.31.

There's many things
that hurt
that sting
our bodies &
our feelings-

Sometime Parents nudge -
try to mold our lines
like kneading fudge
into a mold.

Is the shape
they try
to make
right for you?
or is it fake?

I was a kid
I'm a father now
trying to do his best somehow
with Mom, with Theo, with you.
Holy Cow!

Have fun today!
Loveeee
Dad

Balancing love, pride, concern and frustration—that's what being a father is. I'm always bouncing back and forth between those feelings (and more), sometimes more than one of them at a time. What to do? How to make love always come out on top? Always just love you and Joanna for who you are, and not worry about whether or not you're all you could be—all I want you to be? Is that the way? I believe that at the end of the day that is the key. I have to push and prod and hope and dream and help out along the way, but in the end I ultimately just have to give you my unconditional love. You got it Theo! But it doesn't mean I won't tell you when I think you're making a mistake.

Note to Theo, February 27, 2008 (age 16, 11th grade)

Wednesday, February 27, 2008

Dear Theo,

Balancing love, pride, concern, frustration—that's what being a father is. I'm always bouncing back and forth between those feelings (and more,) sometimes more than one of them at a time. What to do? How to make love always come out on top? Always just love you and Joanna for who you are, and not worry about whether or not your all you could be — all I want you to be? Is that the way? I believe that at the end of the day that is the key. I have to push and prod and hope and dream and help out along the way but in the end I ultimately just have to give you my unconditional love. You and Theo! But it doesn't mean I won't tell you when I think you're making a mistake.   Love,
Dad

human after all

Notes expressing disappointment and anger, and saying sorry

AT TWENTY-EIGHT YEARS OLD, with a newly minted master's degree, I found myself living back at home with my parents. I was spending nearly all my days revisiting my childhood as I culled through piles of notes, when I felt compelled to look at my mom and dad and say, "I'm sorry." I was deep into reading through the notes from my middle school years and could hardly stand to continue.

"For what?" my mom replied when I made my seemingly earnest apology.

"For being so obnoxious and ungrateful," I said, holding a stack of notes in my hand. "I read through all this and feel like I was such a brat. I was so angry, apparently sad, and clearly didn't show appreciation toward you guys the way I should've."

My parents simultaneously laughed and, with sincerity, told me I was crazy—for many reasons, namely that they were both still in the honeymoon phase of having their adult daughter living back at home with them (I'm serious about that). But aside from the joys of being together again, they also told me I was unfairly targeting my past—every preteen and teenager struggles to juggle the onset of puberty, endless friendship drama, and increasing school pressures. Plenty juggle more than that. And, more often than not, those struggles can manifest into "brattiness," blown-out arguments, and unfair blame flying around the home. Though not everyone's nightmarish behavior is documented as thoroughly as mine, I wasn't the first kid to show an inadequate appreciation for the roof over my head.

I still cringe when I read an especially difficult note— one where my dad tries his best to grasp what made me *so angry* at my family, or wonders how we can possibly find a way to *talk without arguing*. It's difficult to read and see, plainly on the page, how hard he was trying to reach me, to stay optimistic, to promote love, and how much I seemed to just not care.

> Feelings like this don't go away quickly. Finding the truth in situations like this is not easy. The surface facts only tell that . . . The surface. They don't go deep to the reasons, the feelings behind the actions that cause the eruptions, that cause the responses. It takes a lot of work and time to figure them out. But it's worth the work and time to try.
>
> Note to Joanna, January 13, 2000 (age 11, 6th grade)

A hard love is what we have. It's love but it's hard. Hard to put up with sometimes. Hard to take and not give it back the same way. Hard to even see the love through all the mess, the stress, the frustration, the disillusionment, the regret, but it's there. It is and you know it. Don't be afraid to show it. Don't blame and point a finger. Feel the love inside and find the smile.

Note to Joanna, December 18, 2001 (age 13, 8th grade)

I don't think Theo or I were uniquely underappreciative of our parents, but our dad was unique in his willingness to engage with our frequent states of frustration, moodiness, rudeness, and general teenage disinterest in family. He met us both where we were with his words and revealed his own vulnerabilities, wrongdoings, and insecurities along the way in order to level the playing field. So sometimes, I find myself moving from feeling bad about these notes to feeling reflective when I stumble on thoughts that aren't just about Theo and me being difficult, but instead about the universality of human trial, human error, human misunderstandings, and human regrets.

I want to say we all make mistakes and it's important that we forgive each other, and just as important that we forgive ourselves.

Note to Theo, November 3, 2005 (age 13, 8th grade)

I'm a man—a human being—and I happen to be your father. I'm not always right. I'm not always appropriate. But I always want to be. I always try to be. I sometimes fail. I'm sorry for that. I love you more than my words could ever express. I want for you more than your share. I pray for you every day.

Note to Joanna, December 17, 2001 (age 13, 8th grade)

Over the years, mornings would come when there had been a disagreement the night before—maybe a door was slammed, biting words were shouted across the dinner table, or someone came home in a cranky mood. These notes range from "big deals" to smaller moments that highlight the daily imperfections and realities we all experience. In these moments, my dad would often question if he and my mom were doing a good job as parents. He wasn't afraid to analyze his own efforts as our dad and acknowledge places where he should've been, or could still be, better. And he was never afraid to say "I'm sorry."

Note to Theo, November 17, 1998 (age 7, 2nd grade)

I'm sorry for losing my temper last night. Sometimes I realize what a difference there is between what kind of person I think I am and what kind of person I really am . . . I'll try to be a better dad! All a father wants his kids to know is how much he loves them. How much I want you to be the best you can be. How much joy I feel for you when you succeed and how much pain I feel when you fail. How anxious I am that you do your best and that your best is rewarded with success. I guess I want a lot . . .

Note to Joanna, February 25, 2003 (age 14, 9th grade)

Often, verbal disagreements between two people can be blown out of proportion in the moment. Because of the routine of Bob's writing, he would find himself reflecting on these disagreements from a new vantage point—early in the morning, after a night's sleep, with a cup of coffee. As he sat and wrote on days like this, he'd ask us to think about what had happened the night before with similarly fresh eyes, to examine how we acted in hindsight, and then ask us to view our respective problems with perspective, maybe in a different light, or perhaps just learn that we should approach a conversation differently next time.

When you want something ask for it—don't make everyone guess what you would like. You might not always get what you want, but a lot of times you will. Plus then other people will know what you like or don't like and we will give you what you like sometimes without you asking . . . Help us make you happy by using words to tell us about you.

Note to Theo, May 7, 2001 (age 9, 4th grade)

While my dad was constantly communicating with us through writing, he was self-conscious about how we all talked and acted together in person. He felt like he was better at putting himself on paper than presenting himself at the table. It's a topic that he touches on in the notes, and one that many would find perplexing—given the depth of topics he brought to light every day in our hands. Because he didn't consider himself a good communicator, the notes would often touch on how we all needed to work to talk *to* each other, and *with* each other, more than *at* each other.

> People say hurtful things sometimes without meaning to or even being aware that they are being hurtful. Sometimes we're tuned to a certain "hurt" frequency and we pick up on it, sometimes we're not so sensitive and it flies right by. Causing hurt is a two way street. Many times someone hurts us and we hurt that person or some innocent person right back. "What goes around comes around." Try to spread good things around and good things will come right back at you!
>
> Note to Theo, February 22, 2006 (age 14, 9th grade)

> It's so easy to be misunderstood. Isn't it? We all feel like no one really understands us . . . We can't really feel the way our words and deeds affect another person. We can only see things from our point of view. It's a struggle— a noble struggle—to really try and understand people. To see the world the way they see it. The only thing for all of us to do is struggle on.
>
> Note to Joanna, October 18, 2004 (age 16, 11th grade)

Learning and growing is a fact of life that never ends—or should never end. My dad believes that passionately. Just because he was the parent in these situations didn't mean he believed he was fully evolved, complete, and right at all times. We were all growing up and maturing together.

> I can see you struggling with some feelings that are "different" for you. I see Theo dealing with feelings that are "different" for him. I feel like these past few years I'm dealing with "different" feelings myself. Feelings about my life—where it's going—how fast it's going—what I'm doing to make it what I want—to make it better for me, for my family. We all constantly are struggling with different things. It's a part of life. Do your best to understand yourself and grow. You'll be fine!
>
> Note to Joanna, February 17, 2000 (age 11, 6th grade)

Our notes are filled with lessons derived from the little hiccups of life, of parenting, of growing up, of being a sibling, of being a child. And they always end with a reminder that despite it all, we are all human, and there is still love to spread around.

Our lives together have ups and downs. Days when everything seems "right" and beautiful—days when it's all wrong. Sometimes it's just moments of rightness or wrongness. I can be in a bad mood and not even realize it—saying things in a not-nice way and not being able to help it. Understanding later on what I was feeling and doing. Does that ever happen to you? Probably so—you are human after all. I'm sure it happens to all of us. Communication is the key! It's the answer. It's what helps us get through. Talk to me. Help me. And I'll help you. Because I love you.

Note to Joanna, April 28, 2000 (age 11, 6th grade)

Hey Joanna Ruth

Our lives together have
ups and downs.
Days when everything seems
"right" and beautiful —
days when it's all wrong.
Sometimes it's just moments
of rightness or wrongness.

I can be in a bad mood and not
even realize it — saying things
in a not nice way and not being
able to help it. Understanding
later on what I was feeling and
doing. Does that ever happen to
you? Probably so — you are human
after all. I'm sure it happens to
all of us.

Communication is the key! It's
the answer. It's what helps us get
through. Talk to me. Help me. And I'll
help you. Because   I Love You
                          Dad

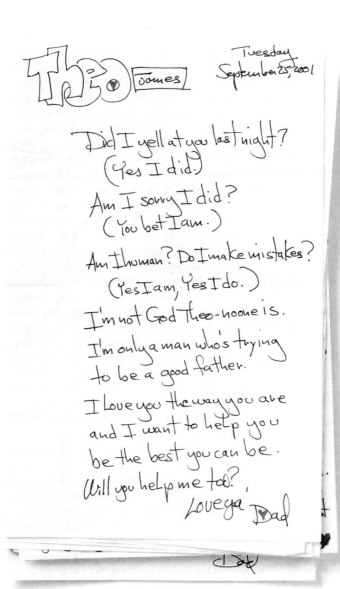

Note to Theo, September 25, 2001 (age 10, 5th grade)

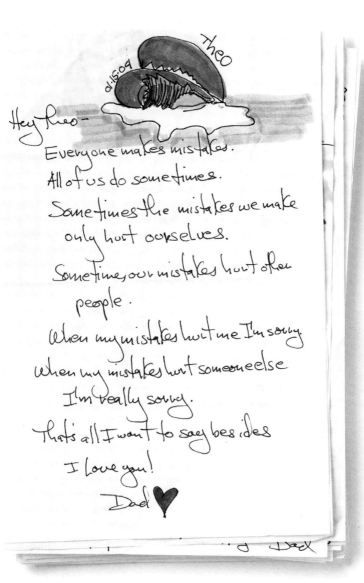

Hey Theo—

Everyone makes mistakes.
All of us do sometimes.
Sometimes the mistakes we make
    only hurt ourselves.
Sometimes our mistakes hurt other
    people.
When my mistakes hurt me I'm sorry.
When my mistakes hurt someone else
    I'm really sorry.
That's all I want to say besides
    I Love you!
        Dad ♥

Note to Theo, January 15, 2004 (age 12, 7th grade)

Cooperation. Appreciation. Consideration. Understanding. Patience. Love. How do you teach these qualities? I guess by embodying them myself and teaching by example. When you look at Mom and I do you see us cooperating with each other? Do we seem to appreciate each other? Are we considerate? Do we try to understand each other? Are we patient? Do we show our love? We are all human. These are human qualities—and so by definition they are imperfect. We <u>intend</u> to demonstrate all these good qualities all the time but we fail because we are human. But we try! That's what people do—they try to be perfect in the way they live their lives. They try knowing they will fail to some extent. Because if you don't try, you fail completely. I don't expect you to be perfect. I just want you to try your best!

Note to Joanna, November 4, 2002 (age 14, 9th grade)

Hey Joanna Ruth -

Monday
November 4, 2002

Cooperation
Appreciation
Consideration
Understanding
Patience
Love

How do you teach these qualities? I guess by embodying them myself and teaching by example. When you look at Mom & I do you see us cooperating with each other? Do we seem to appreciate each other? Are we considerate? Do we try to understand each other? Are we patient? Do we show our love?

We are all human. These are human qualities and so by definition they are imperfect. We try to demonstrate all these good qualities all the time but we fail because we are human. But we try! That's what people do - they try to be perfect in the way they live their lives. They try knowing they will fail to some extent. Because if you don't try you

[written vertically along right margin:] stand a complete chance you will be perfect. That's true & you only get your best! Love, Dad

[written at bottom:] ♥ ♥ Dad ♥ ♥

More than anything I hate being misunderstood. Do you know what I mean? Like people assume something about my words or actions that isn't anything like what I meant. I hate that! There's so many things in our lives that are hard to control and that's one of them that bugs me. Some of it is my own fault because expressing my feelings is hard for me. When you don't talk about your feelings much, then of course other people have to guess at what's going on inside—and they frequently guess wrong. So opening up more would help. Another funny thing is that even though I hate people "guessing wrong" and making assumptions about me—I find myself making assumptions about other people. Communication is key!

Note to Theo, February 28, 2007 (age 15, 10th grade)

Wednesday
February 28, 2007

Dear Leo
my son ♥

More than anything I hate being mis understood.
Do you know what I mean? Like people assume
something about my words or actions that is not
anything like what I meant. I hate that! There's
so many things in our lives that are hard to control
and that one of them that bugs me. Some of it
is my own fault because expressing my feelings is
hard for me. When you don't talk about your feelings
much, then of course other people have to guess at
what's going on inside. And they frequently guess wrong.
So opening up more would help. Another funny thing is that
even though I hate people "guessing wrong" and making
assumptions about me - I find myself making assumptions
about other people. Communication is Key! Love,
Dad

Sometimes we open our mouth when we should have kept silent. Oftentimes we leave a friend waiting for words we never say. Sometimes a situation cries out for action, yet we fail to see and act. Other times we run off half cocked and promptly fall on our faces. Some mistakes we notice, we regret, while other ones we remain blissfully unaware. It's always better to see, understand and learn. Forgive yourself and move on.

Note to Joanna, February 16, 2005 (age 16, 11th grade)

Wednesday
February 16, 2005

Hey Jo 93   Good Morning

Sometimes we open our mouths
when we should have kept silent.
Othertimes we leave a friend waiting
for words we never say.
Sometimes a situation cries out for
action yet we fail to see and act.
Othertimes we run off half cocked
and promptly fall on our faces.

Some mistakes we notice, we regret
while other ones we remain
blissfully unaware.
    It's always better to see, understand
& learn. Forgive yourself and
move on. I love you so much!
                Dad ♥

Did I tell you...

MY DAD IS the type of guy who cries at movies. Like, practically every movie. His favorite is *It's a Wonderful Life*, and no one teases him for crying during that one. But I will forever crack a smile when I think about us going to see *Pokémon the Movie*, looking over, and hearing him sheepishly say—"What?! Come on. Ash turned to *stoooone*. Is he going to come back?!" I don't remember much from my Pokémon-obsessed days, but I do remember that.

In a 2017 *New York Times* interview with Jay-Z, the rapper says: "The strongest thing a man can do is cry. To expose your feelings, to be vulnerable in front of the world. That's real strength."

In a letter to a friend about meeting my mom back in the late seventies, my dad writes: *Being vulnerable is a part of loving, not a weakness, but a strength.*

Clearly Bob was ahead of his time.

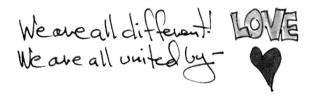

We are all different! LOVE
We are all united by—

Throughout the entire collection of notes, my dad shares who he is, how he thinks, and why he loves. Sometimes the notes were written simply to say "I love you," and other times they went much further than that. They discussed what love is—how it manifests itself, is identified, evolves, and what it might mean to us at any given age. They talked about who we love—each other, our extended family and friends, favorite sports teams, pets, neighbors, and strangers. And they underscored the guiding principles and age-old questions of love—Why does the emotion exist? Why is it worthwhile? Why should we try to seek it out, every day, and work on growing it?

> Fun, love and work—is that life or what? All three necessary components to a healthy life. Love is the hardest to find. If you're lucky, you're born into love—family love, and you at least have that. Finding love outside your family is not easy. It's not that it's hard work, like digging a ditch, but neither can you just go online and type in "soulmate" and hit enter either.[1] Finding love is one thing. Recognizing when you meet it is another. And keeping it, growing it, is another still. It takes fun and work to make love.
>
> Note to Joanna, April 2, 2003 (age 14, 9th grade)

---

1. Internet dating has obviously changed significantly since 2003 . . .

My dad displayed his sensitivity and vulnerability more to us on those pages than he did in any movie theater. Every day he would hand each of us a piece of paper that served as a little magnifying glass to peer inside of him. Who he was as a person in his own right—aside from being a dad—was always changing and growing, but he still allowed us to take a look. At times we'd find a man filled with spirituality, and other times someone with deeper skepticism. Sometimes he felt driven and rewarded by work, and other times he struggled to find value and passion in his chosen career. There were times when my parents' marriage was strong and comforting, and other times when they would struggle with their differences. Regardless of the day, month, or year, however, he would show us his love. And he gave that gift to us with the knowledge that Theo and I might not be ready to return the favor in the same way just yet, but he always believed in the promise that we would.

> Every single person alive today (and whoever has or ever will live) has to have faith—faith in themselves, faith in God, faith that the sun will come up in the morning, faith that they will have time in their lives to accomplish what they want—there are all kinds of faith. I've been writing you notes every school day since you could barely read and I do it with the faith that they mean something to you (like they do to me) and that you read most of them (maybe all, who knows?)
>
> Note to Theo, February 22, 2007 (age 15, 10th grade)

There is a case to be made that every note within the collection could be categorized as a note about love. Much of what he was sharing, and working to express, was his own love—how that love feels, looks, is tested, and expands. And just like all our notes end with some form of "Love, Dad," most of our days, then and today, include a moment when he looks at a member of my family and says, with genuine uncertainty and a smile: "Did I tell you I love you today?"

> Did I tell you I love you today and every day?
> Good days, bad days, always. Did I?
> Did I tell you yet today?
> Well I do—I did—I always will!
> Note to Theo, March 8, 2001 (age 9, 4th grade)

> You know honey that I love you always! You know that—I know you do because I feel your love too. I take it with me wherever I go. That's the beautiful thing about love. You don't have to have the object of your love right next to you to know it—to feel it—inside. I'll be with you today and every day.
> Note to Joanna, October 29, 1999 (age 11, 6th grade)

To think my dad could ever believe that he hasn't sufficiently expressed that sentiment may seem ridiculous. And when he poses this question, often the response from one of us includes a laugh alongside our "Yes, of course you did." But regardless of whether he said *I love you* once, twice, or more, he was committed to promoting the cause of his love and repeating the sentiment again and again, in as many different ways as he could muster.

> I'll never stop loving either of you. I'll love you and be with you forever. A poet once said there are many kinds of love in the world—but no two loves are the same. Scientists say that no two snowflakes are the same either. I guess that's one reason I love watching snow fall . . . And one reason I love you too!
>
> Note to Joanna, March 19, 1996 (age 7, 2nd grade)

Sometimes these sentiments felt "mushy," embarrassingly over-the-top for a middle schooler to digest, so I would blush and roll my eyes to a friend if they managed to sneak by my side to read along. I was often sheepish about sharing the especially sweet declarations. But in hindsight, the lessons on love that are woven into so much of his writing could not be more important to revisit, reconsider, and share.

> I know the word "Love" might not be cool to a 12 year old boy. It probably wasn't too cool to me at your age either. But just think about it sometimes, to yourself.
>
> Note to Theo, December 16, 2003 (age 12, 7th grade)

> For fifteen and a half years I've held a special place in your life—in your heart. You've certainly held a special place in mine. I try to show my love for you every day and I hope you've caught just a hint of it from time to time. I know that someday, maybe soon, other men will

come and earn your heart, at least a place in it. And while your love for him may feel complete—I hope there will always be room for Dad.

Note to Joanna, February 14, 2004 (age 15, 10th grade)

Being in love, and having love in our lives, is something to be thankful for. It also is something that can be terrifying to share because of exactly the vulnerability that my dad—and Jay-Z—embrace. As we grew older and had experiences with friends moving away, entering our first young romances, or watching family members pass on, he wanted us to understand that there are many kinds of love in the world, and some of them can be fleeting.

> Human beings are a fragile collection of systems that work together and bring life to matter. We are born, we love—we pass that love along in our children, and at some point, we die. The pain of losing someone you love is more than balanced by the joy they brought while they were alive. The more people you love in your life, the more joy and sorrow you will have. Don't worry about the sorrow—live the joy!
>
> Note to Theo, October 12, 2006 (age 15, 10th grade)

> How strong our capacity for love is also how strong is our potential to hate. It's risky to love. It's risky because as good as it feels you know that when (if) things go wrong, then it will be equally painful.
>
> Note to Joanna, October 21, 2004 (age 16, 11th grade)

At the same time, he believed that love—the same love that causes pain and suffering—is still worth it. I suppose he is a genuine romantic, tried and true, driven by the belief that the world can and should be a good place, because there is love.

> I want for you to love yourself first and then take that love outside and share it with others.
>
> Note to Joanna, January 10, 2006 (age 17, 12th grade)

Theo

Tuesday
12·16·97

A·candle
burns
For·you
always

Love
Dad

Note to Theo, December 16, 1997 (age 6, 1st grade)

Note to Joanna, January 23, 1996 (age 7, 2nd grade)

Note to Theo, October 20, 1999 (age 8, 3rd grade)

When I'm not with you—when I'm at work or out with friends—I carry you in my heart "hotel." In a place where there's only you! Everyone I love has their own room in my heart "hotel." I only have to think of you and all my love comes to the front—I smile a warm, glad smile and I love. It helps sometimes to remember the people you love—and who love you too—are always as close as your heart hotel—and all you have to do is think, remember and love!

Note to Joanna, November 7, 1996 (age 8, 3rd grade)

Hey Jeanna   Thursday 11·7·96

When I'm not with you —
when I'm at work — or
out with friends —
I carry you in my
    heart "hotel"
In a place where
    there's only you!
Everyone I Love
    has their own
    room in my heart "hotel"
I only have to think of you
    & all my love comes
    to the front —
I smile a warm, glad smile
    and I Love —
It helps sometimes to remember
the people you love — and who love
you to — are always as close as
    your heart hotel — and all you
have to do is think, remember
    and Love!

Love,
ya
Dad

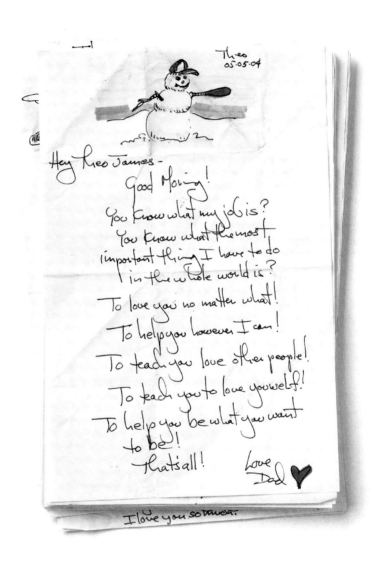

Note to Theo, May 5, 2004 (age 12, 7th grade)

Monday 12·08·'03

A quilt of love. A warm, cozy blanket of love to wrap around yourself and keep you safe. Happy? Can a wrap of love make you happy? Keep you happy? I think it can help with that but happiness takes more than the love of others. It takes love of ourselves. Why? Because love exists between two people or it doesn't exist at all. Each person brings love to the table and together they make a feast. So bring it on Joanna. Feel the love inside you and serve it up generously. I love you so much! Dad ♥

Note to Joanna, December 8, 2003 (age 15, 10th grade)

No one ever said that growing up is easy. No one ever told me that as a kid and it's still not easy even as an adult. I'm still learning how to deal with successes and failures, the good things that I want to happen and the bad things that I wish would just go away. Living encompasses it all—the good and the bad, the happy and sad, the young and the old, the love and the pain—all of it. It can't be any other way. And the only way for us to keep an even keel—a steady course—a balance in our lives—is to understand ourselves, love ourselves, and try our best to love each other. Forgive ourselves the mistakes we make—learn from them—forgive other people the mistakes they make—even when they hurt us—and live each day to the fullest. Know that some days it will be easy and some days it will be seemingly impossible—and just go on—keep on being yourself and trying. Trying to live. Trying to love.

Note to Joanna, January 8, 2002 (age 13, 8th grade)

Hey ♡ Joanna Ruth.

No one ever said that growing up is easy. No one ever told me that as a kid and it's still not easy even as an adult. I'm still learning how to deal with successes and failures, the good things that I want to happen and the bad things that I wish would just go away. Living encompasses it all - the good and the bad, the happy and sad, the young and the old, the love and the pain - all of it. It can't be any other way. And the only way for us to keep an even keel - a steady course - a balance in our lives - is to understand our selves - love ourselves - and try our best to love each other. Forgive ourselves the mistakes we make - learn from them - forgive other people the mistakes they make - even when they hurt us - and live each day to the fullest. Know that some days it will be easy and some days it will seem impossible - and just go on - keep on being yourself and trying. Trying to live. Trying to love. I love you ♡ Dad

Take a moment, every day—even if it's just one, but at least one—take that moment, in that moment remember you are well loved. And after you have taken a moment to remember that you are so well loved, take another moment to reflect on those that you love as well. Your mom, (me maybe?), your sister, GG, your aunts, uncles and cousins—certain friends can find themselves included on your list. Remember that loving someone doesn't automatically mean they will love you in return. You have to earn love, and even then, sometimes your loving them is still not enough. Love is hard and love is sweet.

Note to Theo, February 14, 2007 (age 15, 10th grade)

Wednesday
February 14, 2007
Valentine's Day

Dear Theo
my Son ♥

Take a moment, every day - even if it's just one, but at least one - Take that moment in that moment remember you are well loved. And after you have taken a moment to remember that you are so well loved, take another moment to reflect on those that you love as well. Your mom (me maybe?) your sister, GG, your aunts uncles & cousins - certain friends can find themselves included on your list. Remember that loving someone doesn't automatically mean they will love you in return. You have to earn love, and even then, sometimes your loving them is still not enough. Love is hard & Love is sweet.   Dad

friends and family feels

Notes about family and friends—
how we make them, treat them,
and keep them

I WORE A WHITE PANTSUIT and clear jelly sandals to
my First Communion. The first girl of record at Saint Boni-
face Church who dared to make a fashion statement on such
an important and holy day. I was in second grade at the time
and had recently decided to go with a shorter haircut so that
I no longer had to worry about getting hair in my face while
playing sports. That year I made the choice to stay playing in
a baseball league rather than joining the softball team with
my girlfriends; even after an umpire tapped me on top of
my catcher's helmet, looked down, and said: "You wearing
a cup, son?" I also started playing the drums at age seven,
picked up snowboarding, and would deny to the death that
I had a collection of baby dolls hiding under my bed.

This is the type of kid I was around the time my dad
started writing me notes.

Theo, at age four, was a Power Rangers– and Ninja Tur-
tles–obsessed preschooler. He had a shaggy bowl cut that

made him look like a mini member of the Beatles. He loved wearing tiger-striped suspenders and Air Jordans, collecting Beanie Babies and baseball cards, and donning superhero costumes. When his Montessori school put on an Indian celebration, Theo was put in charge of the mango lassi table. He took his job seriously and asked my parents for an authentic Indian suit to wear, specifically one fitted with a Nehru collar and pearls. Shortly thereafter, he began to ask for garam masala on all his food. Coupled with my dad's stint as a macrobiotic in the mid-nineties, we found ourselves eating a lot of curry and kale for dinner . . . well before that would be considered "so Brooklyn."

Theo and I were in the throes of growing up; we were learning about ourselves, making mistakes, identifying our interests and hobbies, complaining about the brussels sprouts on our dinner plates, and figuring out how to share the different parts of our personalities with others—especially with our friends. Still today, I have many of those longtime friends around me and can reminisce with them about that norm-breaking pantsuit, or the "female cup" I purchased after the umpire incident.[2]

My dad has hardly any friends who knew him during elementary, middle, or high school. That is, friends outside of his siblings.

He's not lacking in the ability to reminisce, however.

---

2. My dad took me to our local sporting goods store to purchase said female cup. Despite these accessories being tailor-made for boys and men, we found something that would provide my anatomy some protection so that if an umpire asked about my nether region again I could reply with a simple: "Yes."

Left: Note to Theo, November 6, 1995 (age 4,
kindergarten). Right: A family picture by photographer
Mary Elmer-DeWitt, 1995.

When we were little kids, we'd ask our dad to regale
us with stories of growing up in a family of eight kids. We
wanted to know more about when he and Uncle Jim went
down to catch minnows in the lagoon behind their home
in Florida and nearly scooped up a water moccasin. Or
about how the siblings used to walk down to the seawall in
Jacksonville to jump into the Atlantic Ocean, all while my
grandma (we called her "GG") prepared dinner. Or that
time when five-year-old Uncle Rick was playing cowboy
in the back of the car on the Garden State Parkway. He
managed to not only lasso the door wide open and roll out
of the moving car, but he also miraculously survived to tell

the tale. Or the other infamous family car story about when they accidentally left nine-year-old Aunt Ellen at a gas station during a cross-country move. They always traveled in two cars—my Aunt Marcia, the oldest, driving her VW Bug with a couple of kids, and GG and Grandpa Frank in their Ford station wagon with the rest. When they packed up to leave after the pit stop, Marcia obviously thought Ellen was in the Ford with her parents, and her parents, well, they assumed she had hopped in the Bug with Marcia.

Scene from a classic Guest family road trip. Bob is on the far right eating french fries. To his right are Uncle Frank and Aunt Ellen. Aunt Joni appears to be tumbling out of the driver's seat window, with Uncle Steve right behind her. Uncle Jim's back faces the camera, and Uncle Rick is behind GG—who takes a break from her cheeseburger to confirm the head count.

These stories were fanciful to us; they were so far from our own experience in a less-chaotic family of four that they felt like *Hardy Boys* fiction. We'd spend nights listening to stories before bed, enjoying what, to us, seemed like the greatest book around.

These family stories were also sprinkled throughout our notes. He'd reach back to tell us about the past because it was exciting, but also because it taught us about our family. We learned about GG's siblings (she was also one of eight kids), our seventeen aunts and uncles, and twenty-four first cousins who were spread across the country. We learned from these stories that families are complicated—and ours is big—and that amid all the craziness (and near-death experiences) comes a closeness that we should not underestimate. He wanted us to know that while we may only have each other as siblings, we had so much more family within reach that could (and should) provide us with the opportunity to build our own precious memories filled with unique experiences, laughter, and fun.

> What a complicated tapestry we weave—from the moment of our birth to our last breath. So many people we meet and even the least of them shape us somehow by our contact. The really big people in our lives— our family mostly and then our friends—shape us in incredible ways. Through it all the colored threads of ourselves form and re-form over and over, gradually taking on a shape that is unique, that is our life.
>
> Note to Joanna, June 2, 2000 (age 11, 6th grade)

Theo and I spent our entire childhood in the middle of New York, one of the largest cities in the world. While we were in a city with more than 8 million people, we both attended the same, small neighborhood school from first grade through senior year. Our friends come from the pool of people we share history with. They could be people we inherently love, like siblings and cousins, who grow up by our sides. Or they might be the kids in the neighborhood or at school, the ones we meet through common classes, school trips, chess clubs, and sports teams. Because we never moved around like our dad, we went through the various phases of growing up with many of the same peers—we had friends that stretched back a decade by the time we were twelve.

Our friendships spanned many years and many evolving interests: from the bands we created to play Alanis Morissette songs at the third- and fourth-grade "Rock-Fest" to the awkward phases of Truth or Dare at bar and bat mitzvahs, and from the years when we all became exceptionally obsessed with academics to the evenings when we'd dodge our parents by meeting up in Prospect Park on Fridays after school. In many notes, my dad shared the important lessons about the different shapes and sizes of friendship, while also reminding us that—like love—these relationships very well might change along the way, and we should never stop giving them our all.

Note to Theo, May 14, 1998 (age 6, 1st grade)

You don't have to go anywhere for a friendship to change. You can't help growing up. You can't help who you are. You can't change what you like to do—what you care about, what you like to talk about. All the many things that make up "you." And your friends can't help it that they grow up—who they are—what they care about—what they like. People grow! People change!

Note to Joanna, November 2, 1999 (age 11, 6th grade)

A friend is interested in the other person's life and is supportive of them. You can lean on your friend. You can count on their help, but only if they can also lean on you and count on your help. Friendship is a two-way street, meaning sometimes you give to your friends, and sometimes they give back to you.

Note to Theo, September 28, 2004 (age 13, 8th grade)

My dad, like anyone, sometimes ponders the "what-ifs" of life—what if he had pursued a career as an artist? What if my parents had moved us down to D.C. to be closer to my grandma? What if he had lived in one town his whole life? What if he were an only child?

> Life is funny Theo. You are born in America, in a big city in 1991 and you have one set of experiences. And those experiences shape you like you are made out of clay. Different experiences, different shape. It's not quite that simple, but almost.
>
> Note to Theo, November 30, 2000 (age 9, 4th grade)

> I think about this stuff sometimes—everyone does—but they're questions that have no answers. We all only get one life—one set of circumstances to claim as our own—to do the best we can with. No second chances at growing up . . . We are who we are and we are who we make ourselves. We all make the best choices we can. Some turn out better than others, but all are aimed at making ourselves and our loved ones the best we can be.
>
> Note to Joanna, November 12, 2003 (age 15, 10th grade)

He enjoys thinking through these unanswerable questions—not because he lives with regrets, but because he understands that we only get one life, and it's interesting to consider how we might be different if we, let's say, grew up on a farm in Iowa (one of his favorite hypotheticals since my grandma and three of my cousins had that experience). Through understanding what our own experiences are and have been, we begin to see how we came to be and can compare and contrast that life with others. We don't know where we would be had things gone another way, but we can invite other people with different pasts to share in life with us.

> Make a friend with your smile. Keep a friend with love. Show happiness to all the people you meet and happiness will come back to you always.
>
> Note to Theo, December 17, 2001 (age 10, 5th grade)

> Understanding comes from relationship, it isn't objectively quantifiable. A thought is read and it strikes a chord or it passes through in silence. A painting appears before you and the meaning you draw from it is up to you. Music, sculpture, architecture, writing, or another human being. What you get from them depends on what you bring to them.
>
> Note to Joanna, March 2, 2005 (age 16, 11th grade)

While our childhoods differed substantially from our dad's, his notes consistently display common ground by discussing friends and family through a set of key tenets: sharing, comfort, understanding, care, and—of course—love.

Hey Joanna Ruth   Tuesday
                                    02·08·00

It's hard being the
oldest kid in a
    family. People really
expect you to set an
    example for the younger
ones. To show, with your
words and actions the
"right" way to act - to
treat other people - to
share - you name it. It's
not easy I know. Nothing
is easy in life - or rather
a lot of very important things
are not easy (but so worth it!)
So try Joanna! Try for mom
and I - Try for Theo & Try for yourself.
Keep it up! Love Dad

Note to Joanna, February 8, 2000 (age 12, 7th grade)

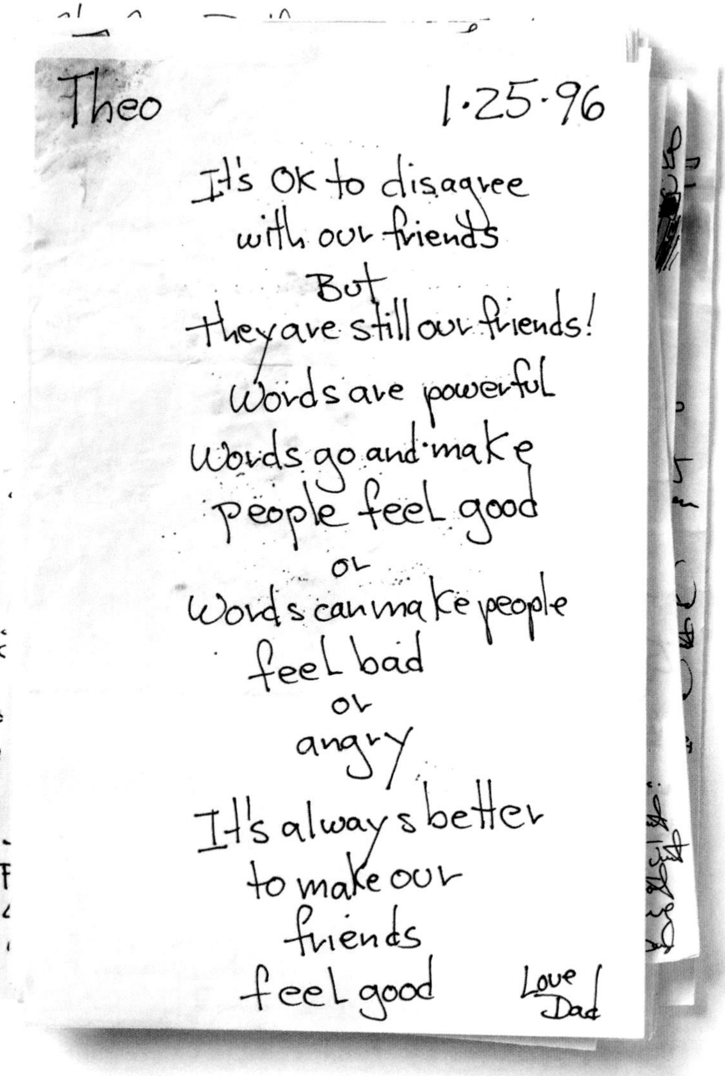

Theo 1·25·96

It's OK to disagree
with our friends
But
they are still our friends!
Words are powerful
Words go and make
people feel good
or
Words can make people
feel bad
or
angry
It's always better
to make our
friends
feel good

Love
Dad

Note to Theo, January 25, 1996 (age 5, kindergarten)

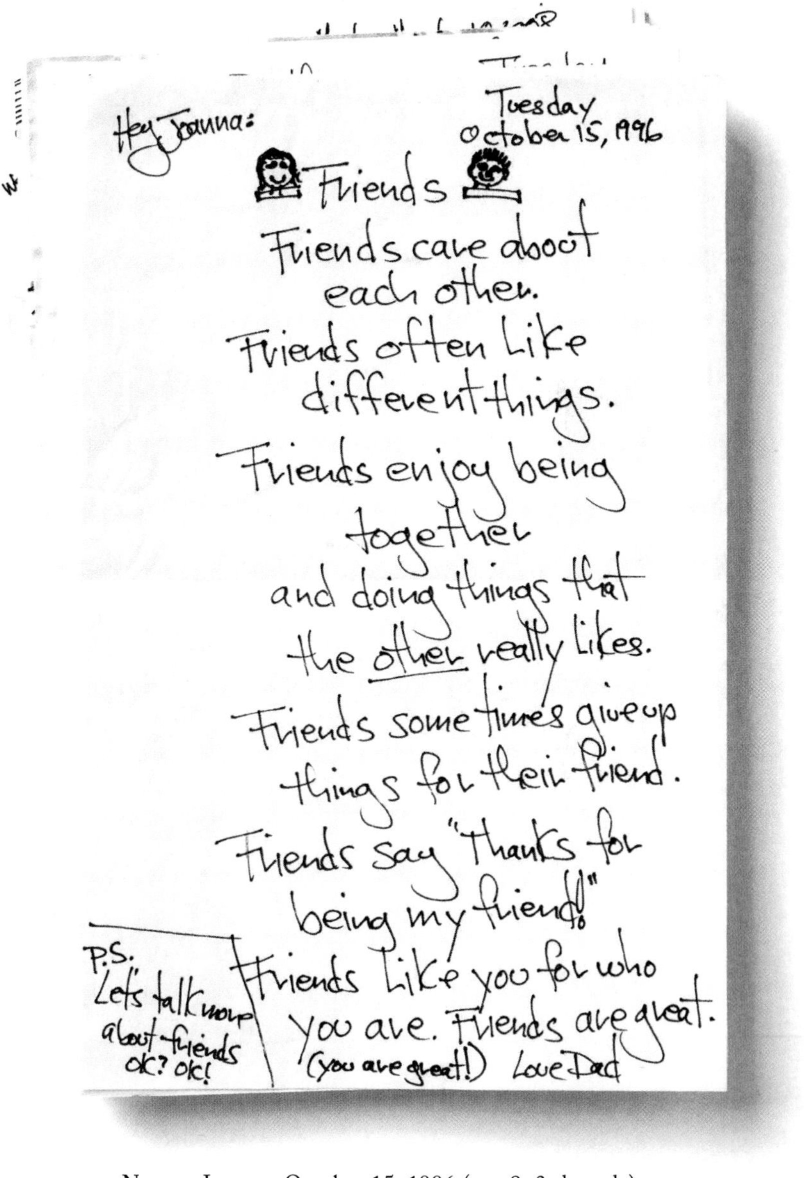

Hey Joanna:

Tuesday
October 15, 1996

Friends

Friends care about each other.

Friends often like different things.

Friends enjoy being together and doing things that the other really likes.

Friends sometimes give up things for their friend.

Friends say "Thanks for being my friend!"

Friends like you for who you are. Friends are great. (you are great!) Love Dad

P.S. Let's talk more about friends ok? ok!

Note to Joanna, October 15, 1996 (age 8, 3rd grade)

What is a friend? Someone you share your feelings with. Someone who cares about you and who you care about. Someone you like to be with, who makes you feel comfortable, safe. Someone you'd do anything to help. Someone who trusts you to keep a secret. Someone you can laugh with. Someone who can laugh at you and it doesn't hurt. Someone who you know is not perfect, who knows you're not perfect either and it's okay. Someone you can cry to. Someone you would defend and who would defend you. Someone who would never make you do something if it wasn't good for you. Someone who encourages you to be yourself, to be your best. Someone you support whenever you can. Someone you make sacrifices for and who sacrifices for you too. Someone you forgive when they hurt you cause it happens.

Note to Joanna, March 31, 2003 (age 14, 9th grade)

Hey Joanna Ruth ♥ ☮ ♥ u   Monday
                              March 31, 2003

What is a friend? Someone you share your feelings with. Someone who cares about you and who you care about. Someone you like to be with, who makes you feel comfortable, safe. Someone you'd do anything to help. Someone who trusts you to keep a secret. Someone you can laugh with. Someone who can laugh at you and it doesn't hurt. Someone who you know is not perfect, and who knows your not perfect either and it's okay. Someone you can cry to. Someone you would defend and who would defend you. Someone who would never make you do something if it wasn't good for you. Someone who encourages you to be yourself, to be your best. Someone you support whenever you can. Someone you make sacrifices for and who sacrifices for you too. Someone you forgive when they hurt you cause it happens. I love you so much! Dad

I've been thinking about my mom the past few days. Thinking about all the things she did for me and my brothers and sisters, to help us grow up right. Guiding me with her example. Working her butt off to make our home life special, which was not easy with 8 kids, a father often away at sea and no money to boot. But somehow she gave us all the gift of love. Your mom is working to give you that same gift—Love. She's working to help you see how good you can be if you only try and believe. She's working to show you the way to be the best you can be. She's loving you with all her heart. Love her back Theo. Show her your love by listening, trying, believing, learning and succeeding. She's holding up her end of the deal, now you hold up yours OK!?!!

Note to Theo, October 27, 2005 (age 14, 9th grade)

Dear Theo   Thursday
                             October 23, 2005

I've been thinking about my mom the past few days. Thinking about all the things she did for me & my brothers & sisters, to help us grow up right. Guiding me with her example. Working her butt off to make our home life special which was not easy with 8 kids, a father often away @ sea and no money to boot. But somehow she gave us all the gift of Love.

Your mom is working to give you that same gift - Love. She's working to help you see how good you can be if you only try and believe. She's working to show you the way to be the best you can be. She's loving you with all her heart. Love her back Theo. Show her your love by listening, trying, believing, learning and succeeding. She's holding up her end of the deal now you hold up yours OK!?!!

I love you, Dad

A house is turned into a home by the people who live in it. All the people contribute to make it a place of refuge, love, growth, security, comfort and more love. The stress of our lives can, from time to time, make it appear to be none of those things. Hopefully that's a short-lived phenomenon and it returns to its true meaning of love and comfort. Change happens no matter where you are. Change is the one constant in life. Every day we wake up to a different world as a different person capable of all things good or bad. We don't always think about that. We don't always think period. Perspective on ourselves is the hardest most necessary thing to achieve. Home is a place to find yourself, hone yourself, be yourself, share yourself, and love yourself—the way I love you!

Note to Joanna, October 31, 2005 (age 17, 12th grade)

Dear Joanna

Monday
Halloween
Oct. 31, 2005

A house is turned into a home by the people who live in it. All the people contribute to make it a place of refuge, love, growth, security, comfort & more love. The stress of our lives can, from time to time, make it appear to be none of those things. Hopefully that's a short lived phenomenon and it returns to it's true meaning of love and comfort. Change happens no matter where you are. Change is the one constant in life. Everyday we wake up to a different world as a different person capable of all things good or bad. We don't always think about that. We don't always think period. Perspective on ourselves is the hardest, most necessary thing to achieve. Home is a place to find yourself, hone yourself, be yourself, share yourself & love yourself — the way I love you! Dad

A family is like the pocket the quarterback moves in, looking at his options, unhurriedly releasing his pass with the best possible chance of success. A safe haven, a sheltered cove to anchor in to plan your next journey out on the open sea. There's a time to lounge and relax in the safety there, and there's a time to use that safety to free your mind and your time to plan and work and grow. I was impressed at your parent-teacher conferences on Friday. Impressed with the appreciation for you that all your teachers showed. Room for improvement yes, but still plenty of success. Keep it up Theo.

Note to Theo, November 10, 2008 (age 17, 12th grade)

Monday, November 10, 2008

A family is like the pocket the quarterback moves in, looking at his options, unhurriedly releasing his pass with the best possible chance of success.

A safe haven, a sheltered cove to anchor in to plan your next journey out on the open sea. There's a time to lounge and relax in the safety there, and there's a time to use that safety to free your mind and your time to plan and work and grow.

I was impressed by your parent-teacher conferences on Friday. Impressed with the appreciation for you that all your teachers showed. Room for improvement yes, but still plenty of success. Keep it up Theo. Love, Dad

teams work together

Notes about sports and teamwork—
how to win and lose gracefully,
and why we practice

WHEN MY DAD CAME HOME one day and told my mom that he wanted to begin coaching my Little League team, she looked at him (he remembers it as incredulously) and said: "How on earth will you do that?? You don't know anything about baseball!"

Sure, he knew the basic rules of the game and was clear on the objective to score more runs than the opposing team. But he grew up never playing any competitive sports, or becoming a fan of any particular team (my mom, on the other hand, spent much of her childhood perched in right field at Yankee Stadium next to her dad, brother Paul, and sister Kiki. Both girls would attend games in their home-made jerseys, sporting a pin on their right chest in sup-port of—and in lust for—their all-time favorite player: #9, Roger Maris). While Bob learned about group dynamics through growing up in a family that could field a baseball team solely with siblings, he wasn't trained in how to teach the fundamentals of any sport. Without the background of what it was like to be coached; without the knowledge and strategy you acquire from watching your favorite team over and over again; without the experience of being up at bat, down by a run, with two outs in the ninth—my mom was, let's say, skeptical that he had it in him.

But Coach Bob he became. So as I was learning how to use two hands to field a grounder, to be a team player, to value practice, and to understand that losing wasn't the end of the world, so was my dad. As Theo and I were putting on pinstripe jerseys to wear to school and as articles appeared in *The New York Times* titled "It's No Contest as Jeter Captures Rookie of the Year," my dad, too, was learning what it meant to be a fan. Sports (especially baseball) were something that we dragged him into, and ultimately, taught him to love.

Derek Jeter/Yankee Shortstop

Note to Theo, October 23, 1996 (age 5, kindergarten)

Sports are a funny thing. Somebody wins and somebody loses and it's great to be on the winning end and it really hurts to lose. It's like a lot of things that you put your heart into—great potential for joy or sorrow. But what's your option? Not play and you don't risk the pain, but you lose out on the joy as well.

Note to Joanna, May 6, 2004 (age 15, 10th grade)

We were kids growing up in New York, and the Yankees were our team. The mid-nineties were a fun time to share a city with the boys in the Bronx, so I can't take too much credit for my dad becoming the fan that he did. Over the years, our notes served to not only deliver poignant messages, lessons, and love, but also to do the simple and fun things, like recap the end of the game we missed after going to bed, illustrate an over-the-wall catch by Bernie Williams out in center field, and highlight the big hits of our favorite players. These notes serve as historical commentary of our fandom. Reading through them brings me back to the joyous dynasty years, when everything went so well, while also forcing me to revisit 2004, when everything went so wrong. (I won't expand further than that; I realize not everyone is a Yankees fan).[3]

---

3. The Yankees and Red Sox faced off in the 2004 American League Division Series. Notoriously, after winning the first three games of the series and leading by one run in the ninth inning of Game 4, Mariano Rivera (uncharacteristically) blew the save. The Yanks lost the next three straight games to their archrival. And my brother and I were served our first taste of heartbreak.

It was fun walking over the Brooklyn Bridge and seeing the parade with you, Theo, mom and Molly. A pretty special team—a pretty special time to be a New Yorker! I'm glad we went!

Note to Joanna, October 30, 1996 (age 8, 3rd grade)

Our family heading over the Brooklyn Bridge to the Yankees Ticker Tape Parade, October 29, 1996.

We have been so lucky to be fans—to become fans— at the time we did. We caught the wave at its peak and the ride has gone on for six years now. History tells us it won't go on forever. Will you still love them when they lose? That's a tough question—shouldn't be, but it will be. It's hard to stay rooting for a loser. But losers need love too you know!

Note to Joanna, October 26, 2001 (age 13, 8th grade)

My dad often wishes he'd had the opportunity to play on a team of his own while he was growing up. He understands that there are larger lessons to be derived from participating in sports, from improving skills both individually and as a member of a group to helping out your teammates, becoming a leader, and working toward a common goal with others by your side. So instead of playing, he learned how to coach us in sports like he did in our notes, and ultimately (similarly) became our number one fan—living vicariously through our plays on the field and on the court.

Hey Theo, do you like to win in sports? Do you? Well then listen up and I'll tell you how. Ready? Here's the secret . . .
1) Practice—you can never be "good enough"!
2) Share your game with your teammates—help them—show them. Don't criticize your teammates when they make a mistake and they won't criticize you . . . Because we all make mistakes.

Note to Theo, April 12, 2001 (age 9, 4th grade)

And, just like the rest of us, he, too, got caught up in the despair of a tough loss. He, too, understood that sometimes the desire to win can cloud our best judgment and make us do the wrong thing. He, too, discovered larger meaning and purpose through actively engaging with our teams and watching sports together in the living room. And as he did, he shared with us the lessons that he, too, was learning.

> You give your heart to another person, or to a baseball team, then sometimes you will be let down. How do you handle that? Do you throw away the love because he/they hurt you, or do you give another chance? I know what I do. I try to grow and learn and value the good times all the more.
>
> Note to Joanna, October 21, 2004 (age 16, 11th grade)

> When you're at school, at work, on the mound, when things aren't going right and you don't have your best stuff—that's when your character shows, that's when you have to get mentally tough and not show your frustration and struggles. Reach back inside and find a way through. Prepare yourself as good as you can and study, work, and play with a passion to succeed.
>
> Note to Theo, October 1, 2007 (age 16, 11th grade)

It takes perseverance and time to develop any skill one wants to acquire—whether that's doing well on an algebra test, crafting a sculpture out of clay, designing an art exhibit, delivering a curveball from the mound, or rushing for a touchdown. Whether you're a kid or an adult, it is hard to find positivity and display patience as you absorb the lessons of defeat—but we were constantly reminded of our strengths, taught how to lose with dignity, and encouraged to keep pushing forward.

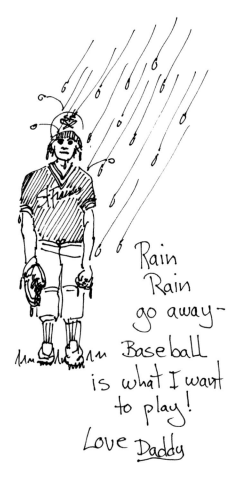

Note to Theo, April 20, 1998 (age 6, 1st grade)

Some notes wished us luck on an upcoming game, while others tried to pick us up from heartbreak, reminding us how proud he was to be following along on our respective journeys to "make something good happen." Through them all, we were told that we could create the best version of ourselves—whether on the field or off—if we continued to work hard, practice, and believe.

> Keep it up front Theo—tip of the brain—"I can do this" is your refrain . . . Everyone who is facing a challenge needs the faith to make it through. Shaun Alexander,[4] when he lines up on the line about to be handed the ball—what do you think is going on in his head? He's reading the defense, looking for holes, and trying to find a spot to make something good happen. That's what we all do every day: try to make something good happen.
>
> Note to Theo, January 31, 2006 (age 14, 9th grade)

---

4. Shaun Alexander is a former NFL running back who played for the Seattle Seahawks.

You know, some days I feel like I have things figured out in my life and other days I feel confused. That ever happen to you? I think it must because it happens to everyone. It's part of being a thinking, feeling creature. Struggle is how we learn. A famous coach once said that you learn more from the losses than you do from the wins. You learn about yourself and what it takes to get up and go at it again. You learn what it takes to win next time. That's what it should be because <u>Life is for Learning</u>!

Note to Theo, February 5, 2004 (age 12, 7th grade)

theo.

Hey Theo James
02·05·04
You know, somedays I feel like
I have things figured out in my life and
other days I feel confused. That
ever happen to you? I think it must
because it happens to everyone. It's
part of being a thinking, feeling creature.
Struggle is how we learn. A famous
coach once said that you learn more
from the losses than you do from the
wins. You learn about yourself and what
it takes to get up and go at it again.
You learn what it takes to win next time.
That's what it should be because life is for learning!
I Love you! Dad ♥

DAD/BOG

Sports! Sports! Sports! It's fun. There's camaraderie with your teammates and that's good. There's discipline and practice—good lessons to learn. But there's something else too—something that [I] missed out on by not playing sports as a kid growing up. That something is challenging yourself to be the best—to be your best—at something. Then believing in yourself—in the skills you've worked to achieve and challenging the other team, the other players, the pitcher when you're at bat, the person guarding you when you're dribbling up court, challenging them to stop you, to get you out if they can. Testing your best against their best. Isn't that why sports is more than just hitting a ball around?

Note to Joanna, October 9, 2002 (age 14, 9th grade)

Hey Joanna Ruhi - ♥   Wednesday
                           October 9, 2002

Sports! Sports! Sports!
It's fun. There's comaraderie with your
teammates and that's good. There's discipline
and practise - good lessons to learn. But
there's something else too - something that
miss out on by not playing sports as a
kid growing up. That something is challenging
yourself to be the best - to be your best - at
something. Then believing in yourself in the
skills you've worked to achieve and challenging
the other team, the other players, the
pitcher when you're at bat, the person guarding
you when you're dribbling up court challenging
them to stop you, to get you out if they can.
Testing your best against their best. Isn't
that why sports is more than just hitting a
ball around?
                    I love you!
                         Dad ♥

Every day is a new day Theo. Every day is another chance to be the best you can be. Be a captain—lead the way to success for yourself and for your friends and teammates. Never give up because you think you're going to lose. Never! If it's your dream to succeed then go out every day and give it your best shot. There will always be tests that surprise you and cause you to stumble—next time be prepared. There will always be games where your shots don't fall or the other team hits you hard—next time be sharper, be smarter—believe in yourself. Believe in yourself and your team. Inspire your team. Be a captain. Be a leader. Be a leader of yourself first and the team will follow.

Note to Theo, February 6, 2007 (age 15, 10th grade)

Thursday
~~Tuesday~~
February 6, 2007

Dear Theo
my Son!

Every day is a new day Theo. Every day is
another chance to be the best you can be.
Be a captain - lead the way to success for
yourself and for your friends and teammates.
Never give up because you think you're
going to lose. Never! If it's your dream
to succeed than go out every day and
give it your best shot. There will always be
feits that umpire you and cause you to
stumble - next time be prepared. There will
always be games where your shots don't
fall or the other team hits your hand. - next
time be sharper, be smarter - believe in yourself.
Believe in yourself and your team. Inspire
your team. Be a captain. Be a leader. Be a
leader of yourself first & the team will follow.
Love, Dad

Teamwork: It's work to be on a team. When teams work together they win. Team: A group of people who play together to win at a sport or competition. Why do you think they call it work? Being on a team is a challenge. You are challenged to be your best and to help your teammates be their best. If you do that—if everyone does that—you will have a winning team. Every team has its share of hot dogs or people who think of themselves as superstars. They go with the competitive nature of sports. All you can do is be your best and try to help everyone—even the "superstars" be their best as well. It's called "sportsmanship." It's called "team first." It's called "leadership." So leave those other feelings off the court. Play as a team. Win or lose, play your heart out and have fun.

Note to Joanna, November 21, 2002 (age 14, 9th grade)

Hey Joanna Ruth, -
Sunday
November 21, 2002

Teamwork - It's <u>Work</u> to be on a <u>Team</u>.

When <u>Teams</u> <u>Work</u> together they win.

<u>Team</u>: A group of people who play together
to win at a sport or competition.

Why do you think they call it <u>work</u>?

Being on a team is a challenge. You are
challenged to be your best and to help your
teammates be their best. If you do that - if
everyone does that - you will have a winning
team. Every team has its share of hot dogs or
people who think of themselves as superstars.
They go with the competitive nature of sports.
All you can do is be your best and try to help
everyone - even the "superstars" be their
best as well. It's called "sportsmanship". It's called
"~~team first~~". It's called "leadership." So leave those
other feelings off the court. Play as a team. Win or lose
play your best and have fun. Love Dad

Losing is always painful. There's only one solace you can take and that's knowing that you did everything you possibly could to prepare yourself and you held nothing back from your all out effort. If they are going to beat you, let them have to beat the best "you" there is. In sports they often say that the team that "wants it" more than the other wins. You know all this stuff—that you have to believe in yourself, you have to have the right attitude, concentration and effort. You know that. But knowing and doing are two different things. So don't put it off. Do what has to be done now because tomorrow may be too late. Then losing will really hurt.

Note to Theo, February 26, 2008 (age 16, 11th grade)

Tuesday February 26, '08

Dear Theo

Losing is always painful. There's only one solace you can take and that's knowing that you did everything you possibly could to prepare yourself and you held nothing back from your all out effort. If they are going to beat you let them have to beat the best "you" there is. In sports they often say that the team that "wants it" more than the other wins. You know all this stuff. That you have to believe in yourself, you have to have the right attitude, concentration and effort. You know that. But knowing and doing are two different things. So don't put it off. Do what has to be done now because tomorrow may be too late. Then losing will really hurt.

I love you!
Dad

Finding Success

Notes about working hard, with reminders to believe in yourself, have the right attitude, and accept encouragement

NOTES WRITTEN IN THE MORNING, before kids race off to their school days, naturally contain messages about educational success. We received notes that praised the hard work we put into a project, congratulated us on a well-written essay, encouraged us to keep trying after a poor test grade, and ones that recommended ways that we could survive a particularly difficult class or teacher. But more often than not, the notes that centered on learning and working hard highlighted lessons that were more broadly applicable to finding success in life—academically and beyond.

> There are two options facing you when confronted with a new problem or decision in your life. You can say: "This looks tough—let me get going!" Or you can say: "This looks tough—I could never do this!" That's it! It doesn't matter whether it's climbing a mountain or solving a math problem. Yeah, maybe sometimes you'll come to realize that you took on a challenge that you

just couldn't handle or solve—but take it on first. Then
if you fail, you can still be proud of yourself for trying.

Note to Joanna, December 18, 2001 (age 13, 8th grade)

My dad never thought much about being a great student growing up. It's unclear as to whether or not this was
due to the frequency with which he changed schools, or
the fact that he listened to his older brothers when they
told him that teachers only read the first and last pages of
any essay you submit (N.B.—This was *not true* then, nor
is it true today). Probably all these things played a part,
but perhaps most important was that he hadn't identified
what he *loved* yet. He didn't embrace the work that he felt
passionate about—being an artist—until his early twenties,
after an ill-advised stint at Clemson University, where he
enrolled as a pre-veterinary science major. Taking organic
chemistry was an unpleasant (yet efficient) way to discover
that this would not be his chosen path.

So sometimes our notes included traditional sentiments
about doing well on school papers and exams—study hard,
do the research, take your time, relax—but more often they
were about what it takes to do well in *anything*. He wanted
us to understand that we could (and should) learn to enjoy
learning. He taught us that learning was not only a valuable,
lifelong pursuit, but that it could also be fun. He reiterated
again and again that the most important successes we could
find were success in love, friendship, and family, along with
the pursuit of knowledge, our hobbies, and our passions. If we
were willing to devote the time it took to learn about ourselves
in the moment, we would surely be rewarded in the future.

As much as I want you to do well academically, I want you to have a productive, happy, fulfilling, long and love-filled life. Proportion! A sense of proportion. It's hard to have in the day-to-day moments of our lives. Pull back once in a while and look at your life. Be sure you have your goals straight and then readjust them if they're off and dive back in.

   Note to Joanna, April 30, 2002 (age 13, 8th grade)

It's good to try and know yourself. Try to avoid the simple but mistaken idea that you already have a fixed idea of who you are. You're growing and changing every day. Every day there are new possibilities. Try to be open to them and learn about yourself!

   Note to Theo, September 14, 2007 (age 16, 11th grade)

One day my mom told me that sometimes my dad would get into bed at night and say: "Do you think Joanna [or Theo] read my note today?" He would be genuinely concerned as they discussed whether or not he was reaching us the way he intended. He never followed up with, "Maybe I shouldn't write the notes anymore," but rather, "What can I do to make her [or him] understand me? Want to hear from me? Trust me?"

Aside from this news breaking my heart, I think I know now why he'd ask those questions. It wasn't because he felt the action of writing to us was futile, that it wasn't "worth it," or that he even felt like we *had* to read every note he did write. (After all, the experience was as much about him processing through his own thoughts as it was about us getting the opportunity to read them.)

But as he sat in bed after evenings when Theo or I seemed especially down or angry, worrying that we hadn't read what he wrote that morning, he wanted to know what he could do differently to communicate the most important message he had to deliver: just do your best; I will love you no matter what.

> At peace is a hard place to find in ourselves because we like to get down on ourselves for our imperfections. Just realize that you are growing, Joanna. You'll make mistakes along the way, and you'll do things incredibly right too. I'll love you either way!
>
> Note to Joanna, June 11, 2002 (age 13, 8th grade)

> When you succeed, I will love you. When you fail, I will love you. If you try your hardest, I will love you. If you give up, I will love you. Sure, I have hopes for you—how could I love you and not want things for you? You're living your life. No one else's. So when you succeed, you get to feel great, and when you fail, you get to feel bad. Which feeling do you want more?
>
> Note to Theo, October 17, 2005 (age 14, 9th grade)

As I was reading through Theo's notes from high school for the first time, I noticed illustrations of the acronym **A.C.E.** spread across many pages. **Attitude**, as described in one of these notes, means *a good attitude—a good outlook—an understanding of what's going on and an acceptance of what you've got to do to deal with it.* **Concentration**, he wrote, is the demonstrated drive to focus on a goal *and concentrate with all of your ability.* Once you accept this challenge with the right attitude and concentrate on what you have to do, then you can give your best **Effort**. Highlighting this acronym became my dad's way to consistently deliver the message that whether we're talking about a baseball game or a chemistry exam, it is always important to focus on improving and fine-tuning the tools and methods at your disposal for learning. He wanted us to understand that we might not strike out every person standing at home plate, or ace every test handed to us, but we could still learn in the face of struggle. If we gave any difficult task our all, we would grow more than we realized, and we would give him all he wanted as well.

> Everything we do involves struggle. Sometimes we win, sometimes we lose. But no matter what happens, we grow. We grow and learn. It all starts with the struggle. It all ends with the growth. Cool hunh?!
>
> Note to Theo, April 9, 2003 (age 11, 6th grade)

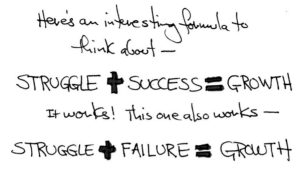

Here's an interesting formula to think about —

STRUGGLE + SUCCESS = GROWTH

It works! This one also works —

STRUGGLE + FAILURE = GROWTH

My dad defines success in a way different from most of academia. He of course wanted us to become good students, but he also wanted us to know that getting good grades was just as important as growing into a reliable friend, a loving daughter, a caring sibling, an interested citizen, and beyond.

> I'm not crazy about the focus of education these days, with the pressure to get good grades and to "test well." To me grades, or the focus of learning on grades, misses the point of education entirely . . . Kids are competitive and I guess you all spur each other on to get good grades. But my point is grades don't measure love of learning. When school is over and the grades are a matter of record, what's left if you didn't learn to love learning?
>
> Note to Joanna, April 20, 2005 (age 16, 11th grade)

Recently, my dad and I were talking about the notes, and he said: "You know, just because I was constantly providing a reminder to believe in yourself didn't necessarily mean that you guys would actually believe in yourselves. It felt like a necessary thing to say, but I have no illusion that it was always helpful. But just because saying it isn't going to automatically result in an 'Aha!' moment for you doesn't mean I shouldn't say it. Over and over again. You're not always shouting into a hurricane as a parent. It's important to say 'you can do it,' whether or not it works. You have to have a reason to believe it might be true." And believe in us he did. Our notes are filled with encouragement and compliments—sometimes he explicitly wrote "You can do it," "I'm proud of you," or "Believe in yourself," and other times he just sent those sentiments jumping off the page.

You'r made yourself as ready as you can be. So go ahead & jump in. The water is fine!

Note to Theo, January 17, 2006 (age 14, 9th grade)

There's no way to know whether or not Theo and I are more successful and "better" people because of the lessons we found inside our notes. We can't go back in time, remove them from our life experience, and see how things might have been different. But my dad can say with confidence that he grew from writing them. He grew from embracing an **A**ttitude that he had something to say. From **C**oncentrating and coming up with lessons, ideas, and stories that would help guide us in the right direction. And finally, from putting in the **E**ffort every morning to share all that and more. Today, he has found different ways to remain engaged in our lives, to deliver these messages, and to remind us that the combination of these lessons, mixed with a dream, is all we need.

> It's easy to be overwhelmed by the realities of life and not do the things you want to do. It's easy to feel like something has to give so you forget about your "like to's" and "want to's" and only do your "have to's." But don't settle for that . . . By all means, do and do well your jobs, your work, your "have to" things—but never give up or push back or forget about the things you love to do as well.
>
> Note to Joanna, December 18, 2002 (age 14, 9th grade)

"Use your head." Ever heard that before? Did you know your brain is like a computer? Imagine what a miracle it is to be able to think. God gave you a brain to use—use it well. Don't be afraid to use it. Don't be afraid to make a mistake. Your brain is a tool—it helps you work—it helps you play. Your brain can learn new things. There's lots of room in there. Mess around! Fill it up! Have fun!

Note to Theo, November 16, 2000 (age 9, 4th grade)

Theo James   Thursday Nov. 16, '00

"Use your head."
Ever heard that before?
Did you know your brain
is like a computer?
Imagine what a miracle
it is to be able to think.
God gave you a brain
to use - use it well.
Don't be afraid to use it.
Don't be afraid to make a mistake.
Your brain is a tool - it helps
you work - it helps you play.
Your brain can learn new things.
There's lots of room in there.
Mess around! Fill it up!
        Have Fun!   Love
                        Dad

I couldn't sleep very well last night. I woke up thinking about what makes people succeed. Succeed in anything—school, sports, business, life. And I decided that the one thing that contributes to success the most, more than natural talent and luck, is a willingness to try and fail and try again. Most of us are afraid of failure so we don't try things, or we don't try our best, or we laugh it off. We don't want to be embarrassed or hurt. It's natural to feel that way—natural but it holds us back. It keeps us from experimenting with new things or from reaching our potential with the things we think we know and like. So fight that fear, Joanna. Try new things. And when it comes to the things you love, fight for them too. Work hard on where you need the work. Recognize where you're weak and work on it. Make yourself better. No one else can do it for you. It's your one life.

Note to Joanna, December 3, 2001 (age 13, 8th grade)

Hey Joanna Ruth -

Monday December 3, 2001

I couldn't sleep very well last night. I woke up thinking about what makes people succeed. Succeed in anything- school, sports, business, Life. And I decided that the one thing that contributes to success the most, more than natural talent and luck, is a willingness to try & fail and try again. Most of us are afraid of failure so we don't try things, or we don't try our best or we laugh it off. We don't want to be embarrassed or hurt. It's natural to feel that way- natural but it holds us back. It keeps us from experimenting with new things or from reaching our potential with the things we think we know and like.

So fight that fear Joanna. Try new things. And when it comes to the things you love fight for them too. Work harder where you need the work. Recognize where you're

[margin, right side:] weak and work at it. Make yourself better. Someone else can do it for you. Love Dad. If you're the one.

HOPE is an amazing and powerful thing! Think about it . . . Where would you be without hope? "I hope I make this shot." "I hope I do well on this test." "I hope I can earn a B average." It's so important to feel hope in all that we do. Yes you have to work hard to try and make sure that your hopes come true, but without hope nothing is possible. Hope for a better future for the realization of our dreams is what makes living and working hard possible. Sometimes our goals seem so far away and out of our reach. Without hope we might give up. Yet it's exactly the time when there seems to be so little reason to have hope that hope is so important to have. Work and hope go hand in hand!

Note to Theo, November 7, 2005 (age 14, 9th grade)

Dear Theo

Monday
November 7, 2005

HOPE is an amazing and powerful thing! Think about it... where would you be without hope? "I hope I make this shot." "I hope I do well on this test." "I hope I can earn a B average." It's so important to feel hope in all that we do. Yes you have to work hard to try and make sure that your hopes come true, but without hope nothing is possible. Hope for a better future for the realization of our dreams is what makes living and working hard possible. Sometimes our goals seem so far away and out of our reach. Without hope we might give up. Yet it's exactly the time when there seems to be so little reason to have hope that hope is so important to have. Work & hope go hand in hand!

I love you Theo. Dad

"Who am I?"

That's the hardest question in the world.

You can't ask anyone else for help. You can't solve it with a computer or a dictionary or a textbook—the answer isn't in any of those places.

The answer is only in one place—in your own heart. It's really in there you know—I'm not kidding. Look and you will find it. Be honest and you might not like what you see. But be true, be hopeful, be passionate, and you will see that that image that you see is always changing. Always evolving, growing, always in the process of becoming. There is never any one answer to the question "who am I?" If you are living, learning, playing, working, then you are growing and changing constantly. Look inside yourself—what do you see? Do you like yourself? If "yes" then keep it up. If "no" then what do you need to change to make the answer "yes"? Start by seeing the good inside and try to add more every day. It really works!

Note to Joanna, September 30, 2003 (age 15, 10th grade)

Hey Joanna -
Good morning!

Tuesday
September 30, 2003

"Who am I?"

That's the hardest question in the world.

You can't ask anyone else for help.

You can't solve it with a computer or a dictionary or a textbook - the answer isn't in any of those places.

The answer is only in one place - in your own heart. It's really in there you know - I'm not kidding. Look and you will find it. Be honest and you might not like what you see. But be true, be hopeful, be passionate (sp?) and you will see that that image that you see is always changing. Always evolving, growing, always in the process of becoming. There is never any one answer to the question "who am I?". If you are living, learning, playing, working, then you are growing & changing constantly. Look inside yourself - What do you see. Do you like yourself? If "yes" then keep it up. If "no" then what do you need to change to make the answer "yes"? Start by seeing the good inside and try to add more everyday. It really works!
                    I love & believe in you! Dad

Don't be afraid to take chances. Don't be afraid to make mistakes. Don't be afraid to realize you made a mistake, apologize and correct course. Draw a line with confidence and then draw another. Trust your eyes, your hands, your head and your heart. Don't be afraid to lose or you may never win. Take your work seriously. Take yourself seriously. When you do that your "fun time" will be sweeter. Have dreams. Make plans. Make them happen. Take care of your own stuff. Solve your own problems. Think about the problems of others and help however you can. Live your life well.

Note to Theo, February 19, 2009 (age 17, 12th grade)

Thursday, February 19, 2009

94

Dear Theo –

Don't be afraid to take chances. Don't
be afraid to make mistakes. Don't be afraid
to realize you made a mistake, apologize and
correct course. Draw a line with confidence
and then draw another. Trust your eyes,
your hands, your head and your heart.
Don't be afraid to lose or you may never
win. Take your work seriously. Take
yourself seriously. When you do that
your "fun time" will be sweeter. Have
dreams. Make plans. Make them happen.
Take care of your own stuff. Solve your
own problems. Think about the problems
of others and help however you can.
Live your life well.   Love,
                              Dad

What is 100%? How do you give 100% to so many endeavors at the same time? Isn't there only one 100% in each of us? I was talking with your mom this morning about lots of things but one thing that stuck with me is this idea of 100%. To be a 100% good parent, a 100% good spouse, a 100% good boss or employee, a 100% good friend. How do you carve up your one 100% into all these different ones and be 100% in all of them? I guess the answer is you try to do it all—that's all. You just try! So have a 100% good day Joanna. I love you so much (100%).

Note to Joanna, February 6, 2006 (age 17, 12th grade)

Dear Joanna

Monday
February 6, 2006

What is 100%? How do you give 100% to so many endeavors @ the same time? Isn't there only one 100% in each of us? I was talking with your mom this morning about lots of things but one thing that stuck with me is this idea of 100%. To be a 100% good parent, a 100% good spouse, a 100% good boss or employee, a 100% good friend. How do you cover up your one 100% into all these different areas and be 100% in all of them? I guess the answer is you try to do it all - that's all. You just try! So have a 100% good day Joanna. I love you so much (100%)

Dad

contemplative envelope

Notes with metaphors, internal thoughts, philosophizing, and who-knows-where-that-came-from

OCCASIONALLY A NOTE TOOK a trip through the washing machine. This was distressing. At least, it felt that way to Theo and me given how upset our mom would get. We didn't know where the notes were going, but we still felt guilty, like we had been rude through the action of forgetting to take the paper triangle out of our pocket.

There's a note to me from September 2004 that references my "first day of school" note going through the wash. *Mom was devastated and wanted me to remember what I had written and do it again. I can't really do that so I'm just writing you a new note about the first day of your junior year of high school* . . . As I've been working on this project and reading through all our notes, it's become more and more clear just how un-extraordinary (and seemingly essential) my dad viewed his morning ritual. He never thought about how the notes might string together. He didn't put pressure on himself to write something poignant and prescient enough to withstand the test of time (or the wash). And he never thought about skipping a day.

He used each empty page as a cathartic release, as a place to share his top-of-the-mind thoughts—in the same way he used to share his rambling ideas and illustrations on the pages of old sketchbooks, when he was writing for no intended audience.

Reading is like turning the key and starting off on a journey.
Writing is a gift from me to you and you to me–pass it on…
Love is holding onto the back of a bird
as it soars and dips and perches on a sea cliff nest.
Singing is unlocking the door.
Learning is the greatest gift to yourself you can give.

Note to Theo, June 12, 2007 (age 15, 10th grade)

After moving home, I asked my dad if it was okay to sift through boxes of these sketchbooks, and I was glad to have received his stamp of approval as I quickly realized they were part sketchbook, part journal. There were ones from the early days of Pratt, when he was trying to understand the elements of art and searching for his own style. Others from the years when my parents were starting their business, when he was focused on growing a company and finding satisfaction at work. Still others from when Theo and I were young kids, when he was thinking through the beginning, exhausting days of parenthood and trying to balance his career goals with his family priorities. Each book was filled with stream-of-conscious-style writing and crosshatched sketching. And each time I picked up a new one, I was reminded again that expressing himself on the page was the most natural way for my dad to work out the big (and little) aspects of his life.

Illustrations from Bob's sketchbooks. What if we all
were totally, utterly freeeeeeeee?

As he sat down to write our notes, he never had a plan of what exactly he would say, but he did organize himself. Over the years, his style of organization changed—but within many of the writing pads he used, he'd keep a piece of scrap paper. These scraps were (of course) also saved, and scrawled across them were bits of color from testing out new markers, important events to know (*Aunt Kiki's birthday*; *Theo's class trip*), and occasional quotes that might provide inspiration if he got writer's block (*Believe in your future!*). On one of these pages, I found a quote by the writer Henry James: "We work in the dark. We do what we can. We give what we have."

Who knows where he saw this quote from James's short story "The Middle Years," but I've thought about it a lot since reading it myself. To me, it feels like the words reflect, quite literally, what my dad's experience writing the notes was all about. Every morning, he woke up before the rest of us to work in the dark. He did what he could to grapple with and examine himself, his parenting, and who we, as his kids, were becoming. And through thinking about what his love felt like and meant, and what he could do to relay that love to us, he gave what he had.

We work in the dark.
We do what we can.
We give what we have.
Henry James

I looked up this story to understand the quote's context; the paragraph reads: "'We work in the dark—we do what we can—we give what we have. Our doubt is our passion and our passion is our task. The rest is the madness of art.'"

My dad had many doubts on how best to parent, how best to communicate, how best to love. And he wrote to us because the action helped him understand and alleviate that doubt. Through writing he spread his love, he was curious and creative, and he found a place where he could try to express the thoughts that occurred to him during peaceful morning contemplation; and the next day, he could try again. That seems (to me) like the "madness of art" that none of us realized he was making.

The hot, harsh sun filtered through layers of misty water vapor; the ground damp, the sounds muted—slightly hushed. It's the perfect contemplative envelope.

Note to Theo, April 29, 2009 (age 17, 12th grade)

The ritual of note writing was always preceded by a morning dog walk. The time my dad spent outside—listening to the sounds of the morning, the city's natural hustle, watching the sun rise or the snow fall—is often highlighted within his writing. Weather and nature provided a starting point and often sparked metaphors to be drawn out between the patterns outside and the patterns of our lives.

Gray, thundering days have their own special beauty about them. Just like people. Every person has something special about them that makes them beautiful in their own unique way.

Note to Joanna, May 19, 2000 (age 11, 6th grade)

Green grass wet with last night's rain, the sky gray but tinged with pink and blue and the ground around our house covered with pink petals. Take time to notice and appreciate your surroundings. Our world can be such a beautiful place. In your life, help to keep it that way.

Note to Theo, May 2, 2008 (age 16, 11th grade)

And some mornings he just felt like reaching out to explore something else entirely—something abstract—often without a concise end point (*I guess I just felt like rambling today!*). He allowed his mind to wander; to acknowledge where it was on any given morning; to start thinking, and then start writing, and then see what he found.

This morning it was dark when I walked Sunny. Clear, blue sky with some tiny pinpoints of scattered stars. Very beautiful—very peaceful—I was wishing I could hear you play your penny whistle while we walked along.

Note to Joanna, September 16, 1997 (age 9, 4th grade)

It's hard to break out of the comfortable shell we live in, see people suffering, see things that need changing, and decide to do something about it. Be a son, be a brother, be a friend, be a student, be an athlete, be a ceramist, be a lover, be a father, be a changer of things. One hat at a time or all at once or any combination, that's what life is. We are born thinking only of ourselves. Growing up—maturing—is about learning to turn that energy outward to the world.

Note to Theo, January 14, 2009 (age 17, 12th grade)

During the years that I received my notes, I never thought of them as "art." And I had no idea that after one of these little pieces of paper, filled with our dad's energy and love, went through the wash, my mom treated them as such a treasure. She'd carefully remove the disintegrated paper from our pockets, let it dry, meticulously unfold what was left, and then try her hand at piecing it all back together.When I realized there was a pile of these "destroyed" notes amid the stacks I was sifting through, I showed them to my dad. He was especially touched. "I wrote them. You read them . . . It was as simple as that," he said to me. "I wouldn't have even thought to save them. Seeing the ones that went through the laundry—all damaged and destroyed—those ones I really love. For some reason they resonate with me. Like, this was a thing so special, that even this little fragment got saved somehow. Even if all the words are no longer there, this little fragment is left, and it represents the whole thing. I love the idea of that."

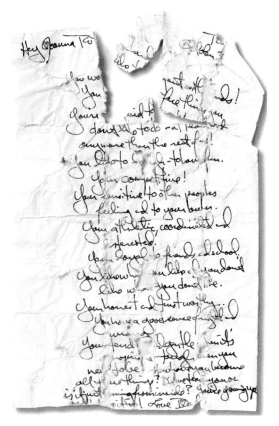

A note that "survived" a trip through the washing machine.

We all have good days and bad days, experience successes and failures in everything we do. The notes were something my dad tried to do, and did dutifully, every day. He never viewed writing them as an assignment, but rather something that he enjoyed doing—doing for Theo, for me, for himself. And he hoped, just like we all do, that he would have more notes that resonated with us than ones that fell flat.

We are who we are even though we do our best to make ourselves into who we want to be. At 50, I still struggle every day to be a better person—to be more like I want myself to be. Some days I succeed better than others. All the days of my struggles merge to form the picture of me. The good days and the bad days blend into a whole. At least that's the way I see it!

Note to Joanna, October 30, 2003 (age 15, 10th grade)

Some mornings the thoughts came with ease—the spark of the flame from a match hit the candle and the words would just flow. Other mornings it was less obvious what to write, what to say, which direction to head—so he would tap into his never-ending stream of optimism, and just try.

What could be better than getting up every day—taking a deep breath, swinging your legs onto the floor and standing up? What could be better than just being young and alive?

Note to Theo, December 8, 2000 (age 9, 4th grade)

TheoJames —

Open your mind Theo.
I know that we all see the
world with our own eyes.
Our own unique eyes.
From the time we are born
our biggest challenge is to
understand ourselves &
to understand that other
people are different from
us - different not wrong.
So learn from other people.
Ask questions and listen
to the answers.
Listen, think & Learn.

Love
Dad

Note to Theo, October 17, 2002 (age 11, 6th grade)

The World Joanna—you can't imagine how beautiful it really is. Think of the different places—tropical islands, snow-capped mountains, deserts of sand, miles and miles of green fields. It's awesome! Think of the kinds of weather—bitter cold—blinding sun—stormy wind and rain—cool breezes—warm winds. It's awesome! Think of the people in the world—black and brown, yellow and red and white—old, young and babies of each. It's awesome! And just think. You get to be here in the middle of it all. So what do you do? You smile— you say "thanks" and you live!

Note to Joanna, November 10, 1999 (age 11, 6th grade)

Hey Joanna Ruth

The World Joanna - you can't imagine how beautiful it really is. Think of the different places - tropical Islands, snow-capped mountains, Deserts of Sand, miles and miles of green fields. It's awesome! Think of the kids of weather - bitter cold - blinding sun - stormy wind and rain - cool breezes warm winds. It's awesome! Think of the people in the World - Black & Brown, yellow and red and white - old, young and babies of each. It's awesome! And just think. You get to be here in the middle of it all. So what do you do? You smile - you say "thanks" and you Live!

love, Dad

One of the hardest yet most important things for anyone to do in their life is to see themselves—see and understand. Understanding yourself is a broad phrase and I mean it in a broad sense. Understanding just who you are, what you believe in. Understanding your limitations yet always trying to expand them and grow out of them. Recognizing that you're changing and attempting to direct that change. Make goals and then work to achieve them—doing what it takes even though it's hard. Shaping for yourself a vision for yourself. Recognizing that you will only have this one life, no second chances to start over, to accomplish those goals. So make the most of each day, each opportunity. Find the joy in growing and becoming Joanna!

Note to Joanna, February 21, 2002 (age 13, 8th grade)

Hey Joanna Ruth -   Thursday
                                February 21, 2002

    One of the hardest yet most important
things for anyone to do in their life is
to see themselves - see & understand.
Understanding yourself is a broad
phrase and I mean it in a broad sense.
Understanding just who you are, what you
believe in. Understanding your limitations
yet always trying to expand them and
grow out of them. Recognizing that you're
changing and attempting to direct that
change. Make goals and then work to
achieve them - doing what it takes even
though it's hard. Stopping for yourself
a vision for yourself. Recognizing that
you will only have this one life, no second
chances to start over, to accomplish those
goals. So make the most of each day, each
opportunity. Find the joy in growing and becoming
Joanna!   I love you   Dad

"On your own two feet!" Ever hear of that expression? Ever thought about what it means? I'm thinking about it this morning because we all have to stand on what we have. God gave us two feet to stand on and he gave us those same two feet to take us where we want to go. Most of us don't think about our feet too much—they're a long way from our head—but where would we be without them? Your feet are strong enough to hold your weight and then some. They're strong and flexible enough to walk you where you want to go—to run and get you there faster if you want. They may be a long way from your head but they'll listen to you and go where you tell 'em!

Note to Theo, January 23, 2006 (age 14, 9th grade)

Theodora

Dear Theo

Monday
January 23, 2006

"On your own two feet!" Ever hear of that expression? Ever thought about what it means? I'm thinking about it this morning because we all have to stand on what we have. God gave us two feet to stand on and he gave us those same two feet to take us where we want to go. Most of us don't think about our feet too much - they're a long way from our head - but where would we be without them? Your feet are strong enough to hold your weight and then some. They're strong and flexible enough to walk you where you want to go - to run and get you there faster if you want. They may be a long way from your head but they'll listen to you and go where you tell 'em! Love, Dad

Sunrise is always such a positive, life affirming time of day for me. A new beginning. The promise kept. The fear of the dark unknown is washed away in the steady oncoming light. Alive. It makes me feel alive. Sometimes what lies ahead in the day's schedule is scary or anxiety producing—but what the hey—it's a new day and another chance. Take the ball and run! P.S. Thanks for the goodnight kiss!

Note to Joanna, November 16, 2004 (age 16, 11th grade)

Tuesday
November 16, 2004

Hey Joanna

45

— good morning —

Sunrise is always
such a positive, life affirming
time of day for me.
    A new beginning. The promise Kept.
The fear of the dark unknown is
    washed away in the steady
oncoming light. Alive. It makes
me feel alive.
    Sometimes what lies ahead
in the days schedule is scary
or anxiety producing but what
    the hey — its a new day
and another chance.
            Take the ball down!
            Love Dad ♥

P.S. Thanks for the good night kiss!

Mornings—school mornings—work mornings—sleep in mornings—up early mornings—dark dog walking mornings—swimming mornings—biking mornings—beautiful blue mornings with incredibly bright crescent moons and a scattering of stars—so crystalline—so beautiful—achingly so—so glad to be alive morning. Decision making seems fresh and possible on mornings like this. God seems in his (her) heaven on mornings like this. It's good to be loved on mornings like this. To feel that love in your bones, in your heart, in your head, in your smile, in the first person you meet on the street.

Note to Theo, September 23, 2008 (age 17, 12th grade)

Tuesday, September 23.08

Dear Niece

Mornings - school mornings - work mornings - sleepin mornings - up early mornings - dark dog walking mornings - swimming mornings - biking mornings - beautiful blue mornings w/ incredibly bright crescent moons and a scattering of stars - so crystalline - so beautiful - achingly so - so glad to be alive mornings. Decision making seems fresh and possible on mornings like this. God seems in his (her) heaven on mornings like this. Its good to be loved on mornings like this. To feel that love in your bones, in your heart, in your head, in your smile, in the first person you meet on the street.

I love you! Dad

times like these

Notes that reflect on moments
in history, newsworthy events, and notes
that wonder about the state we're in

WHEN I BEGAN THE PROCESS of reading through our collection, I imagined that the bulk of the notes would lend themselves to a sort-of oral history of my family. After all, my dad documented nearly every day of our family unit's life for fourteen years. I figured I'd read note after note that reflected on our days, our ups, our downs, our games, our relationships—our notes that emphasized lessons and memories that only applied to Theo and me. I was wrong.

Today, after reading through thousands of notes, I understand that so many of them, written on a specific date, during a specific time in history, are timeless in their lessons. I've realized that this piece of our family story not only describes much of who we were but also continues to teach us who we want to be.

PS.
Last night President
Clinton made his "State of
the Union" address. He
asked everyone in the whole
country to work with him to
take care of each other and
make sacrifices - Do you
know what a sacrifice is?
A sacrifice is when you
give someone else something
that you wanted very much for
yourself.... and you do it
willingly & happily.   Love
                         Dad

Note to Joanna, January 1996 (age 7, 2nd grade)

I've never found the first half of this note, written after one of President Clinton's State of the Union addresses; my guess is this particular speech was delivered in January 1996, as Clinton's first term was coming to a close. The president delivered the speech, and my dad translated the message for my young mind, teaching the value of selflessness and community along the way.

Tucked within many reflections on the day's historical events were these lessons on what it means to be a good citizen. He wanted to make sure we cared about the society around us, that we sought out the good, understood and grappled with the bad, and, in the end, were kind and civil—whether we were seven or seventeen.

You can't find truth if you're not looking for it, and you can't look for it without an open mind. No issue divides cleanly between black and white, right or wrong. Look, listen, and by all means form an opinion. But never stop looking for the truth!

Note to Joanna, November 20, 2003 (age 15, 10th grade)

The notes are filled with sentiments that gave us direction and taught us right from wrong. They're stories of our family and where we came from. They're lessons on love that we didn't know we needed to hear. They're encouraging words we received to take a deep breath before a tough test. They're the optimism we were handed when times didn't seem all that great. And they're made complete, relatable, and moving because of the vulnerability that comes across from someone who was trying to digest what was going on around him—the events that comprised

156

our collective human history in Brooklyn, in the United States, and in the world. The notes reminded us that our dad was a person navigating through life, just as we were.

> We are all men and women, girls and boys of our time. The times we live in are unique in so many ways, yet the issues we must face are the same ones that have been around since the first humans. Love, hate, jealousy, passion, ambivalence, search for truth, searching for what makes you "tick." You and your friends are embarking on the same journey that Mom and I are still on, that our parents and their parents were/are on. Open your eyes. Open your heart. Open your mind and go!
>
> Note to Joanna, March 9, 2004 (age 15, 10th grade)

He frequently faced news of struggle and tragedy on the front page of the morning paper, which seeped into his mind as he began to write. These reflections would sometimes become hypotheticals, about what we might do in a particularly complex or seemingly impossible situation, or how we might responsibly balance the competing demands of our own wants with the world's ever-changing needs.

> Do you ever wonder how other people live? I do sometimes. I saw a picture on the front page of the *Times* of a group of women sitting behind some thorn bushes and waiting for bread from a relief agency. They were chased from their villages by rebels and had nothing but the clothes on their backs. Can you imagine life like that if it happened to you?
>
> Note to Theo, May 5, 2004 (age 12, 7th grade)

Hard to have perspective this morning. I wake up to a radio report of over 5,000 people killed in an earthquake in Indonesia and the sports section tells me that both the Yankees and the Mets won yesterday. How do you reconcile these different worlds and then whistle as you go to work? I don't have an answer for that one. We all do it every day. We numb ourselves to other people's suffering. And we continue to love.

Note to Joanna, May 30, 2006 (age 17, 12th grade)

September 11 was, without question, an especially difficult time for the country, and my dad remembers the event feeling even more personal, defeating, and terrifying as a parent of kids growing up in New York City. There was a unifying cry in the aftermath of the attacks that we would prevail, that the United States would rise again and continue to be a world power. But for my dad, finding his own natural positivity amid the thick fog of terror was a challenge. He knew he still had hope and love, but he also felt troubled and unsettled, so he let himself be vulnerable as he dug a little deeper to find optimism and shine it toward the future.

The thing I want you to think about is that yes, there is hate in our world, but there is also good. Tremendous good. You are surrounded by good people—me, your mom and sissy, your GG and aunts, uncles and cousins, your teachers, coaches, friends, policemen, firemen, store owners—so many people, not just here in NYC either, but all around the world. Remember all those good people and always try to be a good person yourself—like you are!

Note to Theo, September 11, 2003 (age 12, 7th grade)

Today is why we study history Theo. To remember. To learn. To teach. To not repeat the mistakes. To honor the innocent who suffered and to vow never to repeat or allow [others] to repeat these sins. You were only a 10 year old boy when the Trade Towers fell, but try to hold onto the memory. I left my office and went to BC and picked up you and Joanna and brought you home. We watched TV in the living room at the [apartment] and we cried. I called my mother and brothers and sisters to let them know we were all OK, but our world has been and will always be changed.

Note to Theo, September 11, 2006 (age 15, 10th grade)

Writing the notes over the years became natural and therapeutic for my dad. As he looks back on those years of writing, he remembers feeling more and more reflective as the years went on. He would hit strides as he sought to find redeeming messages in the midst of everyday life. Often he pushed us to have our own moments of introspection, even if it was uncomfortable; he wanted us to examine the present, the future, and ourselves as we witnessed the historical events, social movements, and cultural upheavals that occurred alongside our lives.

The world is accelerated. The world is "smaller." Information is everywhere—accessible to everyone. Finding what "fits" you the best is a challenge in the best of times. Is it the "best of times" right now? There's a lot to figure out and 20 years from now it will be you and Theo and your friends who have to keep it going. The more you learn about yourself the better person you will be and the more you will help the world.

Note to Joanna, October 18, 2001 (age 13, 8th grade)

Read the paper this morning and I have to say the news isn't good. Not much about Iraq—or even the election right now—it's all about Wall Street, the Bank Collapse and the credit squeeze . . . It's important to not close your eyes to what's going on around you but at the same time, no matter what, you have to stay optimistic and keep the faith. Trust that things will work out all right as long as you keep working hard and believe.

Note to Theo, September 19, 2008 (age 17, 12th grade)

He ultimately believes, and always has, that problems can be solved. Even difficult problems. There are solutions and lessons we learn as we live our lives and are faced with unexpected tragedies, natural disasters, and seismic shifts in our politics. In his notes, our dad did his best to focus on humanity's good, and to emphasize the compassion and care that exists, the love and sacrifice, responsibility and honesty demonstrated by so many people in so many circumstances. He wanted to highlight those moments as often as he could and remind us that we must always make space for these qualities to enter the room.

> I wonder . . . what life could be if we thought about things to do that help others and in return help ourselves. I wonder . . . .

Note to Joanna, September 15, 1997 (age 9, 4th grade)

Theo James

Friday
September 22, 2001

Theo there's a lot of good in the world – Look for it and you will find it!

Theo there's a lot of important work to be done in the world – Open your eyes and look for it – it's there!

Theo there's so much Love in the world – Open your heart and feel it – it's there!

Theo I Love you!

Dad

Note to Theo, September 22, 2001 (age 10, 5th grade)

Hey Joanna Ruth —   Friday
                      September 22, 2001

The world is changing Joanna -
right before our eyes.
Watch, Help, Learn, Grow -
It's really not so different
from what you would do anyway.
The sky is blue
The night is cold
The moon is new
Our love is bold.
While I'm waiting here
This heart of mine is singing
Lover - where can you be.
I don't know why that verse of a
jazz song came into my head -
Maybe it's because it's about a
searching - a longing for love - a
Love that's out there somewhere
in a cold, new world. Look for it
and you will find it Joanna.
                          Love ya
                          Dad

Note to Joanna, September 22, 2001 (age 13, 8th grade)

Today is the one month anniversary of the attack on the World Trade Towers. One month is not a very long time in the big scheme of things, but it still seems like it happened a million years ago. So much of our lives have changed in so many ways in such a short time. Not just for us personally but for the whole country. It's a time to rebuild, a time to examine ourselves—all of us—to see who we are—what do we do to make the world a better place? What do we do to spread love within our family, with our friends, with strangers we meet on the street, with people who feel and act differently than we feel or act? It would be a mistake to believe that we, as individuals, can do nothing to change the world. Believe in the power of love!

Note to Joanna, October 11, 2001 (age 13, 8th grade)

Hey Joanna Ruth -

Today is the one month anniversary
of the attack on the World Trade Towers.
One month is not a very long time in
the big scheme of things but it
still seems like it happened a million
years ago. So much of our lives
have changed in so many ways
in such a short time. Not just
for us personally but for the whole
country. It's a time to rebuild -
a time to examine ourselves -
all of us - to see who we are -
what do we do to make the world
a better place? What do we do to
spread love within our family, with
our friends, with strangers we meet
on the street, with people who feel
and act differently than we feel or act?
It would be a mistake to believe that we,
as individuals, can do nothing to change the
world. Believe in the power of love!   Dad

"She who does not study history is doomed to repeat it." History is so important. Our world today is built on the worlds of yesterday. The knowledge we learn today grows out of the knowledge that came from people before us. You are making new history every day—discovering new things that your children will take and learn from in turn. It's the way the world evolves—people evolve. We are the current result of all the thousands of years of human evolution—scary hunh? Makes you feel foolish sometimes—makes you feel responsible sometimes. In fact it's awesome when you really think about it. So go out there and make some history today!

Note to Joanna, October 2, 2001 (age 13, 8th grade)

Hey Joanna –

Tuesday
October 2, 2001

"She who does not study History
is doomed to repeat it"

History is so important. Our world
today is built on the worlds of
yesterday. The knowledge we
learn today grows out of the
knowledge that came from people
before us. You are making new
history every day – discovering new
things that your children will take
and learn from in turn. It's the
way the world evolves – people
evolve. We are the current result of
all the thousands of years of human
evolution – scary huh? Makes you feel
foolish sometimes – makes you feel responsible
sometimes. In fact it's Awesome when you
really think about it. So go out there and
make some history today! Love ya
Dad

Isn't it funny how America is so evenly divided these days? Why is that? How is it even possible? I heard there's an election for governor in Washington State that, at the last count, had one candidate winning by 42 votes—out of the whole state! Amazing isn't it? For everyone who feels passionate on one side of an issue there is someone equally passionate on the opposing side. It's almost ludicrous. I mean it would be funny if it wasn't so serious. So you examine your views to be sure it's what you believe. You listen to the other ideas because they deserve it too. And you shake your head, laugh, and work for change.

Note to Joanna, December 9, 2004 (age 16, 11th grade)

Thursday
December 9, 2004

Hey Joanne 59

≡≡ good morning glory! ☆

Isn't it funny how America is
so evenly divided these days?
Why is that? How is it even possible?
I heard there's an election for governor in
Washington State that, at the last count,
had one candidate winning by 42 votes—
out of the whole state! Amazing isn't it?

For everyone who feels passionate
on one side of an issue there is
someone equally passionate on
the opposing side. It's almost
Ludicrous (sp?) I mean it would be
funny if it wasn't so serious. So
you examine your views to be sure it's
what you believe. Then listen to the other
ideas because they believe it too. And you shake
your head, laugh, and work for change.   Love Dad ♥

Yesterday a student with a gun killed 32 fellow students in Virginia Tech and nobody knows why. Even if they ever find out some things about his reasons, they will never be able to explain such a horrible, unimaginable act. I think of Joanna away at college and I think of the parents of those 32 kids and I sat here this morning and I cried. How much do I love you and Joanna? How much did those parents love their sons and daughters? Totally! Completely! Unmeasurably! Words can't describe the feelings of a parent for his child. Everyone is somebody's child. Think about that every time you hear about an accident or flood or famine or war death. Everyone is loved. Everyone is special to someone. We are all loved.

Note to Theo, April 17, 2007 (age 15, 10th grade)

Monday
~ril 2007
Tuesday
April 17, 2007

Dear Theo ♥
my Son

Yesterday a student with a gun killed 32 fellow students in Virginia Tech and nobody knows why. Even if they ever find out some things about his reasons, they will never be able to explain such a horrible, unimaginable act. I think of Joanna away at college and I think of the parents of those 32 kids and I sat here this morning and I cried. How much do I love you and Joanna? How much did those parents love their sons and daughters? Totally! Completely! Unmeasurably! Words can't describe the feeling of a parent for his child. Everyone is somebodies child. Read about that everytime you hear about an accident or flood or famine or war death. Everyone is loved. Everyone is special to someone. We all are loved.
I love you Theo! Dad ♥

History unfolds day by day—it never stops—not as long as there are people living on this 3rd rock from the sun. History goes way back to the first humans and continues right up to this very second. The Iraq war will be an important turning point in the history of America and the world—as will 9/11/2001. This is history you're living. Know what's going on around you. Try to see the connection, the causes, the results. We are all connected—all brothers and sisters. Learn to accept and love and not judge your fellow man.

Note to Theo, June 11, 2007 (age 15, 10th grade)

Monday
June 11, 2007

Dear Theo
my Son ♥

History unfolds day by day - it never stops - not
as long as there are people living on this
the 3rd rock from the Sun. History
goes way back to the first humans and
continues right up to this very second.
The Iraq war will be an important turning
point in the history of America and the
world - as will 9-11-2001. This is history
you're living. Know what's going on
around you. Try to see the connections,
the causes, the results. We are all
connected - all brothers and sisters.
Learn to accept and love - don't judge
your fellow man. Love,
Good luck today!   Dad

You know, every morning I read stories in the paper that make me cry. Stories of whole countries full of people being murdered or starved or washed away in floods or dying of diseases. So many people suffering in the world today, while we talk about sports and colleges and new clothes. I'm guilty of blocking it all out as much as anyone else is. It's hard to live your life crying for the whole world. At the same time, it's important to understand how fortunate and blessed we are as a country, as a people, as a family. How many talented people in the world never get a chance to work hard at their dream?

Note to Theo, October 11, 2007 (age 16, 11th grade)

Thursday

Thursday/October 11, 2007

Dear Theo—

You know, every morning I read stories
in the paper that make me cry. Stories of
whole countries full of people being murdered or
starved or washed away in floods or dying of
diseases. So many people suffering in the world
today, while we talk about sports and
colleges and new clothes. I'm guilty of
blocking it all out as much as anyone
else is. It's hard to live your life
crying for the whole world. At the same
time it's important to understand how
fortunate and blessed we are as a country,
as a people, as a family. How many talented
people in the world never get a chance to work hard
at their dream? I love you! Dad

there they go

Notes that process leaving home,
the end of an era

BY THE TIME I was a senior in high school, the notes were well into their "long-form" stage. Full pages—sometimes more than one—of handwriting. Many still highlighted the events going on within our family, touched on various ways to appreciate our successes and learn from our disappointments, and nearly every note included a heart with wings or a butterfly floating around on the page. And as 2006 crept closer, there was a new thought being wrestled with: leaving home.

I was the first to go off to college, deciding after twelve years in the same little neighborhood school that I was ready for big university life across the country. Theo followed three years later, moving out to the Midwest. And during both of our senior years, my dad watched as we assembled our list of schools, sent out applications, had our final sports games, waited for admission letters, and eventually chose where to attend. As he watched, he processed, he wrote, and he savored the moments, imagining what it would feel like, for all of us, to move on.

> You know, how easy it will be to deal with you goin' away to college is not the point for me right now. I'm sure it will be hard for me, but I think I understand something of the natural order of things and I will be able to deal with it. I'm more invested in you right now to worry about me . . . I'm livin' life one day at a time; I'm watching the trees for signs of spring; I'm enjoying these days. I hope you are too.
>
> Note to Joanna, February 16, 2006 (age 17, 12th grade)

> The sun comes up in the morning and it sinks slowly into the west at night. Day follows day in rapid succession. It almost lulls you into forgetting how quickly it's passing by.
>
> Note to Theo, November 12, 2008 (age 17, 12th grade)

He wondered candidly on the page about how he did preparing us for the next step. He questioned the bad and highlighted the good parenting decisions. He commented on the friendships we made along the way. He reminisced about his own experience leaving for college and what it was like to be out on his own. He thought through what our communication with each other might look like moving forward, when the daily notes became a thing of the past. And he kept imparting lessons—about the changes we'd inevitably go through, and how to embrace with enthusiasm the next chapter of our lives.

None of us ever can know what is in store for us in our lives. It's just not possible to know the future. All we can know or seek to know is our own selves and what goals will make our souls grow and expand to our fullest capacity.

Note to Joanna, April 4, 2006 (age 17, 12th grade)

Senior year is one of those big change years—not really boy-to-man, but some of that, plus some home-and-away; watched-over and on-your-own. That kind of thing. It is an exciting time. Live it fully! Enjoy it immensely! Share it freely!

Note to Theo, April 21, 2009 (age 17, 12th grade)

Many of the notes that sent us off during our respective last years at home discussed the unknown and unexpected turns that were still to come, for all of us. This point was made delicately, acknowledging that we would continue to "grow up" through college and beyond, while allowing for us to celebrate the achievements we had made, and the growth that had already transpired and led us to this "end of an era" moment.

> Life isn't always a straight line from point A to point B. It loops de loops and zigs and zags and goes forward and returns. It's the great thing about life I think. You can look back and follow the path, but looking ahead it's only 'til the next turn. Just keep your eyes on the prize and put one foot in front of the other and you'll be OK!
>
> Note to Joanna, May 26, 2006 (age 17, 12th grade)

> Work hard, but have fun at the same time. These next eight months are so important, special, so full of change—make them fit you like a glove. Be yourself now more than ever. Look at the world through your own eyes and trust your instincts.
>
> Note to Theo, January 23, 2009 (age 17, 12th grade)

My dad seemed to understand that the role he played in our lives would change (not diminish . . . just change) when we were no longer so connected in the mundane ins and outs of each other's days. But he didn't harp too much on that; instead he reinforced the key lesson that is so often at the heart of each note: that he, too, was still learning. Even as a fiftysomething-year-old guy, he was, and had been, learning through raising us, through being a husband, through owning a business, through reconnecting with old friends, through walking through new museum exhibits, through coaching our Little League teams and attending our music recitals, through taking us on family trips and having conversations with his own mom. He had been learning right by our side all along.

> You know, the funny thing is that if you do it right, you never stop living your formative years. You never stop learning about yourself, about your interests, skills and goals, about your goals and dreams, your friends old and new, your love, your ability to give and receive love. You really never stop.
>
> Note to Joanna, May 25, 2006 (age 17, 12th grade)

Lots of memories—even at 17 (imagine at 55)—make life rich. Memories of fun things, memories of sad things, memories of people and places—all these things go into our hard drives and affect how we think and feel about the things that happen now and our feelings about the future as well . . . A not-so-famous philosopher once said: "The future's not here yet." How we've learned to deal with things as we grow up either helps us or hurts us deal with things we contemplate in the future. I hope you've learned helpful lessons.

Note to Theo, September 18, 2008 (age 17, 12 grade)

The most surprising thing about rediscovering the thousands of messages within our notes has been how relevant they are to our lives today. The musings he wrote didn't only apply to a specific period of time in our lives, and they rarely touched on outdated issues. We still struggle to communicate our feelings—but we try to express them. We still shout in frustration when we should've spoken softer—but we try to hear ourselves. We still don't believe we can do certain things—but we try to avoid saying "can't." We still have friends who are different from us—but we try to embrace those differences and love them for who they are. We still don't know *what could be better than getting up every day, taking a deep breath, swinging [our] legs onto the floor, and standing up*—we still don't know *what could be better than just being young and alive.*

Go on out there and try things—that's how you learn about yourself and the world. But whatever you try, give it your all, see what's really there, what the limits are, what applications to your life lie inside. Lots of options, most of which may not be appropriate, but don't settle for anything because it's easy, choose it because it's right.

Note to Joanna, May 16, 2006 (age 17, 12th grade)

Each note began on a fresh piece of paper, without the ability to look back on what was said the day before. Events happened during the twenty-four hours between writing, or over the weekends, or during summers, that were lost in the hustle of our every day. Sometimes those events were captured, but often they were not. And instead of always thinking through the lens of the past, my dad saw the page in front of him as his place to express anew and explore the future. He gave each note what he could in an attempt to release his thoughts, test out ideas, discover the unknown, and process the results. And as we neared the end of high school, he tried to bring each of us, himself included, to a place where we could go, and continue to do all of those things, on our own.

> Fly away! And on your way—from time to time—stop and remember! You may have to fight for that extra point, for that extra base, for that drink of water. Be prepared! And when it's your turn—share.
>
> Note to Joanna, January 19, 2006 (age 17, 12th grade)

Dear Joanna—

Thursday
January 19, 2006

FLY AWAY! And on your way—from time to time stop & remember!

You may have to fight for that extra point, for that extra bone, for that drink of water. Be prepared! And when it's your turn—share.

Love,
Dad

As unlike your senior year experience is as compared to my own, one thing is similar. Getting mentally prepared for going out on my own was tough. The things you do consciously and unconsciously to enable yourself to take that step are almost archetypal in their commonness. I want you to know, now that I see it from the vantage point of a father rather than a son, that it's difficult, necessary, important, emotional, and beautiful from this side of the aisle as well. I want to say that I think it's possible to enjoy your last full year at home and still be ready and fortified for the adventure of college life. Our job and obligation as parents has always been to prepare you for this point. How'd we do? I don't really know but I'd say we didn't do too bad! Never be afraid to take a chance, be yourself, and love and be loved.

Note to Joanna, November 1, 2005 (age 17, 12th grade)

36 Dear Joanna

Tuesday
NOVEMBER 1, 2005

As unlike your senior year experience
is as compared to my own, one thing is
similar. Getting mentally prepared for going
out on my own was tough. The things
you do consciously — & unconsciously — to
enable yourself to take that step are
almost archetypal in their commonness.
I want you to know, now that I see
it from the vantage point of a father
rather than a son, that it is difficult,
necessary, important, emotional & beautiful
from this side of the aisle as well. I
want to say that I think it's possible to
enjoy your last full year at home &
still be ready & fortified for the adventure
of college life. Our job and obligation as
parents has always been to prepare you
for this point. How'd we do? I don't really
know but I'd say we didn't do too bad.
We've tried to make a home where you feel & love &
be loved.   Dad

I want for you to discover yourself and to be happy with that discovery—be happy with who you are. I want for you to find new talents in yourself all the time and to find ways to use those talents that benefit you and others as well. I want for you to love yourself first and then take that love outside and share it with others. I want you to understand that people change and grow better through love and support than by criticism. I want for you to understand that friends today will be friends tomorrow if you treat them that way. Yet your heart will never be so full that there won't be room for another and another and another . . . always!

Note to Joanna, January 10, 2006 (age 17, 12th grade)

Tuesday
January 10, 2006

Dear Joanna

I want for you to discover yourself
and to be happy with that discovery —
be happy with who you are. I want for
you to find new talents in yourself all
the time and to find ways to use those
talents that benefit you and others as
well. I want for you to love yourself
first & then take that love outside
and share it with others. I want you
to understand that people change and
grow better through love and support
than by criticism. I want for you to
understand that friends today will be
friends tomorrow if you treat them
that way. That your heart will never be
so full that there won't be room for
another and another and another... always!
Love, Dad

Always there are things worth fighting for. Dreams worth striving for. Friends worth keeping. Strangers worth helping. Lovers worth loving. People worth forgiving. Never stop looking inside yourself for what you are really meant to do. Never stop looking around you for what needs doing. Shake the hand that helps you and offer your hand to help others. Go out the door each morning with your dreams on the tip of your brain and thankfulness in your heart. Work for the things. Want these things. Live for love.

Note to Joanna, January 30, 2006 (age 17, 12th grade)

Dear Joanna

Always there are things worth fighting for.
Dreams worth striving for. Friends
worth keeping. Strangers worth helping.
Lovers worth loving. People worth forgiving.
Never stop looking inside yourself for what
you are really meant to do. Never stop
looking around you for what needs doing.
Shake the hand that helps you and
offer your hand to help others. Go out
the door each morning with your dreams on
the tip of your brain and thankfulness in
your heart. Work for the things. Want
these things. Live for love,

Dad

Workin' hard! Chippin' away at the rock of life. Tickin' off the words, the seconds, the sweat, and the cracklin' synapses. Thinkin' to myself on paper—aimin' my love towards you like a sunbeam—all inclusive, all encompassing—always there for you. Constant as the Northern Star and a whole lot closer. ("Put your arms around me like a circle round the sun.") There's nothing like lovin'—the giving and the getting of it. Soak it in Theo—and never hold back from giving it to whomever [you] feel needs it—wants it, deserves it, returns it. Work hard my son for your future depends on it. It's not a scary thought, it's an awesome one. Grab the bull by the horns and wrestle it to the ground!

Note to Theo, December 4, 2008 (age 17, 12th grade)

Sunday, December 9th, 2008

55

Dear Theo

Workin' hard! Chippin' away @ the rock of life. Tickin' off the words, the seconds, the sweat and the cracklin' synapsis. Thinkin' to myself on paper - aimin' my love towards you like a sunbeam - all inclusive, all encompassing - always there for you. Constant as the Northern Star and a whole lot closer. ("Put your arms around me like a circle 'round the sun.") There's nothing like Lovin' - the giving and the getting of it. Soak it in Theo - and never hold back from giving it to whomever feel needs it - wants it, deserves it, returns it.

Abide hard my son for your future depends on it. It's not a scary thought, it's an awesome one. Grab the bull by the horns and wrestle it to the ground! Love, Dad

What does a man do in uncertain times? In times of decision making? In stressful times of unknown future that seem so important, so necessary, yet so confusing? Where's the compass set on your own true North? Where's your personal GPS? Your Mapquest with the road to your destination all outlined in purple? Well I've got an answer for you—it's right there inside of you. Look around at the options and then look in for the right fit. In the end some choices may seem to be made for you, but that's in large part an illusion because you decide what your options are—what road you want to travel. Look inside and follow your heart!

Note to Theo, February 20, 2009 (age 17, 12th grade)

Friday, February 20, 2009

Dear Theo

What does a man do in uncertain times? In times of decision making? In stressful times of unknown future that seem so important, so necessary yet so confusing? Where is the compass set on your own true North? Where is your personal GPS? Your map quest with the road to your destination all outlined in purple?

Well I've got an answer for you - it's right there inside of you. Look around at the options - then look in for the right fit. In the end some choices may seem to be made for you, but that's in large part an illusion because you decide what your options are - what road you want to travel. Look inside and follow your heart!

Love,
Dad

"Movin' on up!" Headin' on out! We celebrate the changes in our lives as we downshift and ease into the stream of whatever "next step" awaits us. There's a lot to celebrate—a lot of success—maybe some missed opportunities and second guesses in the mix, but all-in-all a steady progress to this point. Not a point as in a pinnacle, but a point along a line, a path, the steady climb you've been on for almost 18 years now. I'm proud of the young man you're becoming and I'm excited by the future man you'll become as you live and celebrate many, many more "points" in the future.

Note to Theo, April 28, 2009 (age 17, 12th grade)

Tuesday, April 28, 2009

125

Dear Theo —

"Movin' on up!" Movin on out!
We celebrate the changes in our
lives as we downshift & ease into
the stream of whatever "next step"
awaits us. There's a lot to celebrate,
a lot of success — maybe some
missed opportunities and second
guess in the mix, but all-in-all
a steady progress to this point.
Not a point as in a pinnacle, but a
point along a line, a path, the
steady climb you've been on for
almost 18 years now. I'm proud
of the young man you're becoming
and I'm excited by the future
man you'll become as you live
and celebrate many, many more "points"
in the future. I love you so much! Dad

I know you decided to take today off and rest after your shoulder injury yesterday, but I didn't want to miss the chance to tell you how proud I feel every time I stand next to you. I watch you and I'm filled with amazement at your abilities, your demeanor, the good looks you got from your mom, your potential to be so much, your tender ways you show your love. Go on! Get outta here!

Note to Theo, April 30, 2009 (age 17, 12th grade)

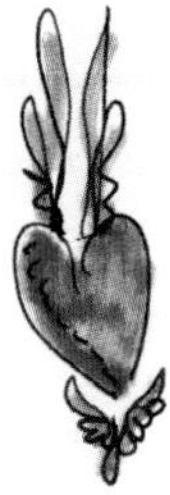

the end

WHEN I LEFT FOR COLLEGE, I brought with me the last daily note I ever received. I remember carefully taping it into an Ikea shadow box frame, worried that I would rip it. That frame has now hung in every dorm room and apartment I've lived in for the last thirteen years. A faded memory of my last day of high school, with a clear lesson on how to live life far, far beyond that.

The note centers on the metaphor of a bridge—the bridge that safely carries you from one place to the next.

It's funny, looking back on the decision to frame that specific note, I realize that my last note was really just the most handy one to bring. I don't remember thinking so much about the message, but rather that I knew where it was, and I wanted to bring a note with me as a reminder of the many that had come before it. I also remember liking that this one in particular had a beautiful illustration of the Brooklyn Bridge spanning across the top of the page. I was a Brooklyn-born-and-raised kid heading out to the desert of Arizona; no amount of memorized Biggie lyrics seemed like they would be enough as I was packing my bags, savoring my last everything bagel, and flying across the country. I wanted that image with me in hopes that I could look at it and feel "home."

I remember bringing it with me for those reasons, and I always find comfort in its presence whenever I look at it hanging on my wall. But now, after re-reading thousands of our notes, I realize that carrying that single note around with me—from city to city—might actually have had more to do with the message on the page than anything else.

The notes can be categorized in a lot of different ways, and viewed from a lot of different angles, by a lot of different people. The lessons drawn from the illustrations, metaphors, and words are often subjective—they allow for individual interpretation, and they allow for that unique interpretation to change, as any reader approaching a note grows older and has new life experiences. But I realize that what they have always been, to me, are the building blocks of that bridge.

Each note helped build a bridge meant to connect my dad with his two kids. They carried his ideas, feelings, personality, and love over to us. They were something he constructed, something he reinforced with new supports, something he worked on dutifully and happily so that Theo and I had something solid to stand on, a path to follow, as we walked through life: from childhood into adolescence, and, eventually, on our way to adulthood. From one state of mind to another.

What a metaphor a bridge is. The connection from one place, one state of mind to another. The path that lets you cross over. Do you need a bridge this summer? What will it be? Summer itself? Time? People? A job? Your family? Walk on out over the water Joanna, just put on your walking shoes and hit the road. Open your eyes while you go. See what you're leaving and where you're going. Remember your way home!

"Last" Note to Joanna, June 8, 2006 (age 17, 12th grade)

Dear Joanna —

Thursday
June 8, 2006

What a metaphor a bridge is!
The connection from one place, one
state of mind to another. The path
that lets you cross over.

Do you need a bridge this summer?
What will it be? Summer itself?
Time? people? A job? Your family?
Walk on out over the water Joanna.
Just put on your walking shoes +
hit the road. Open your eyes while
you go. See what you're seeing
and where you're going.
Remember your way home!

Love,
Dad

Sometimes I'll send my dad some of my favorite sentences from the notes. His response usually falls somewhere between: "Man, who wrote that??" and "Where did I come up with that line?" Occasionally, I'll get an "Amen :-)."

It's hard enough to remember the things you've done when you know you want to remember them years later. It's even harder to remember things you've written when you think those words are going to be read once, hopefully digested, and then disappear into the abyss (read: the trash). But so much of what Bob wrote hasn't been lost in time. The words have been saved, and many of the same sentiments still come flowing from him long since the final note to Theo was penned. He is forever working on that bridge. Whether it has come through the postcards he sent while we were in college, the handwritten birthday cards we get every year covered with the same hearts with wings we used to see so often, the thoughts he shares over texts as he walks through the park with his dog in the morning, or the simple "Did I tell you I love you today?" that we still receive almost every day.

It's that conscious repetition that, from the very beginning, is what mattered so much. The repetitive action of putting pen in hand every day and writing.

Every school day, pen in hand.
I stare at paper and plan
what I'll say today to let you know
I love you so
and the things you think will not sink
but float
like a boat
in our thoughts.

Note to Joanna, May 6, 1996 (age 7, 2nd grade)

At the heart of the whole effort was the idea that an action as simple as saying (at the very least) "I love you," day after day, could accumulate into something more. After all, as he once wrote to Theo: *There's nothing like lovin'—the giving and getting it.* It was that message that never wavered.

And it's that idea of simplicity that rounds out the picture. Perhaps no one but my dad would think of his note writing as a simple action, but his daily routine was second nature to him. And it's the importance of appreciating the simple, natural, everyday things that he wrote about in his "final" note to Theo.

Today is the last regular day of class for the seniors. Is it my last note ever? I can't imagine that it will be. Maybe the last daily one (the simple words are the hardest ones to spell sometimes). Sometimes it's the simple things that are the most special—the most beautiful—the most memorable. Like saying "thank you" and "please." Like taking your earbuds out and listening to the wind and the birds. Like giving a friend a ride, like sharing a good joke, like singing a song in the bath, like snapping off a sharp curveball or connecting on a line drive. Or maybe saying "I love you so much!"

"Last" Note to Theo, May 1, 2009 (age 17, 12th grade)

Friday, May 1, 2009

Dear Theo—

Today is the last regular day of class for the seniors. Is it my last note ever? I can't imagine that it will be. Maybe the last daily one (the simple words are the hardest ones to spell sometimes.)

Sometimes it's the simple things that are the most special—the most beautiful—the most memorable. Like saying "thank you" and "please." Like taking your earbuds out and listening to the wind and the birds. Like giving a friend a ride, like sharing a good joke, like singing a song in the bath, like stepping off a sharp curveball or connecting on a line drive. Or maybe saying "I love you so much!"

Dad

My dad sketched himself and his love onto pieces of paper every day. He wrote how he felt during so many different moments, over so many different years, sharing his unedited thoughts with us without worrying about the occasional spelling errors, run-on sentences, or mixed metaphors. He revealed himself as human on those pages—perhaps in a way that he would not have if he realized the notes would be revisited some day by a different audience. And now that we've taken the time to look back on all that he gave, we can see that it truly was the simplest thing—like receiving a daily love letter from Dad—that was the most special, the most beautiful, and the most memorable of all.

acknowledgments

When you tell people you're going to leave a good, stable job with a 401k and benefits in D.C., shortly after completing a graduate program in Public Policy, to move home to your parents' house in Brooklyn and start "working on a project" about some notes your dad wrote—you end up with a lot of people to thank for not stopping you.

To the folks who got this ball rolling—Scott Menchin, thanks for being my dad's dear friend and understanding his mind enough to believe, without knowing what any of our notes said, that they probably said something beautiful. Tod Lippy, founding editor and executive director of *Esopus*, thanks for not only listening to Scott but envisioning and producing a magazine that perfectly shared our notes with readers for the first time. And to Ann Prescott, our Montessori teacher who suggested that the best way to jump-start Theo's interest in reading might be an occasional lunchtime note from Dad.

To Gail Hochman, who, after receiving her copy of *Esopus* said: "Give me 100 of those notes and we'll make a book." Ten years later, it wasn't so simple, but this process would've stalled if not for your linguistics lessons and determination. While your newest title in my life might be "agent," I'll forever think of you as another mother; in many ways you've helped me become me, and—in no small way—helped this book become this book.

To Deb Futter, Jamie Raab, and the wildly capable team at Celadon Books—you all have embarked on a passion project of your own building a publishing house that is impressive and dutifully cared for. Deb, you have exceeded all my expectations and I firmly believe you will continue to treat my passion project with the sensitivity, pragmatism, belief, and love with which you treat your own. A huge thank-you is owed to Randi Kramer, Rachel Chou, Anne Twomey, Clay Smith, Ryan Doherty, Christine Mykityshyn, Heather Graham, and everyone else in your growing office. I'd also like to thank designer Steven Seighman, production editor Liz Catalano, and production manager Karen Lumley at Macmillan for dealing with my incessant commentary as we turned this elaborate idea into a book. Thanks, finally, to my copy editor, Bethany Reis, and Tamara Staples for the book's photography.

I am blessed with too many sounding boards to count, but a heartfelt thanks is owed to Sian Evans for your willingness to reply to emails with honesty, sensibility, and humor. To Jimmy Ryan, my forever-best-boss, for teaching me that to work for something you love means that being tired won't keep you from working tirelessly. To Isabelle,

Katie, and Chloe, for your endless love, brainstorming, and ability to keep me feeling grounded. To Clare for lending your expert eye and comfy couch. To Stacey (Max) and Liz (Jeff, Leland, Thomas, and William), for adopting me and providing me with four kids who have expanded my heart tenfold. And to Charlie—you are patient and supportive, always down for a catch, and I couldn't ask for more.

The list goes on and on, so I'll just say: To my dearest friends—there's a note where Bob writes: *Treat your friends well and know that there will always be room for one more.* I'd venture to guess a lot of you think I've taken this advice too literally, but I love having each and every one of you— in Austin, Brooklyn, Chevy Chase, Chicago, Northwest D.C., Southeast D.C., Dallas, Denver, Harlem, Harrison-burg, L.A., Maine, Newport Beach, Phoenix, Reno, and the Upper East Side. I wouldn't trade a single one of you for all the money in the world. (And I say that as someone who's lived at home with her parents without a steady in-come for the last two years.)

To my family—I am forever thankful to Nana, Papa, GG, and Grandpa Frank for the ten aunts, seven uncles, twenty-four first cousins, fifteen cousins-through-mar-riage, and twenty-four "other cousins" who are the progeny of those marriages. I would give anything in the world to give this book to my GG, who beamed every time she spoke about my dad and his passion for creativity. And my heart swells as I imagine Aunt Kiki's face had she been able to put a copy of this book on the shelf in her classroom. To all those family members who came before us, and the many more who are to come, I can confidently say I wouldn't be who I am without your love, and I'll never tire of reading *The Relatives Came* and thinking: hey, that sounds a lot like us.

To my brother, Theo—I wanted a little sister so badly that I gave you a Cabbage Patch doll when you came home from the hospital. Despite spending the better half of a decade begging Mom and Dad for another sibling, "only" getting you was the best thing I could've received. You are sweet, unique, handsome, kind, curious, passionate, open, stubborn, gentle, worldly, and literally so many other things that neither you nor I know yet. Thank you for sharing those sides of yourself with me. I love you and will forever cheer from your corner: Go Theo Go.

To my mom, Gloria—I know you think you had nothing to do with all of this, but the truth is you had everything to do with it. You found every note you could. You stored them in a safe place. You moved them all from our tiny two-bedroom apartment into a big old house. Then, when asked if you knew where they were, you said yes. I know, I know . . . I get a lot of "the good" pieces of me from Dad, but I get a whole other half of me from you. You are my everything. You are the person I can't go to sleep mad at. You are the person I speak about most in this world. You constantly remind me that you won't be around forever, but you will forever be an inextricable piece of my heart. Thank you for filling me up.

And to my dad, Bob—you amaze me. And if I'm not mistaken, by the end of this thing, you'll amaze a whole lot of people. To me, being amazed by you is nothing new, yet you find new ways to do so every day. I do my best to never take for granted how lucky I am to call you mine. When I walk around outside, I try to listen to the wind move through the trees the way you do. As I wander through a museum, I try to see colors and lines mingle together the way you do. When I'm feeling frustrated or angry, I try to find positivity the way you do. When I receive something kind from another person, I try to sincerely say "thank you" the way you do. And when words fail me, and I don't know how to properly acknowledge all it is you have given me, I guess the only thing left is to say it how you do: Did I tell you I love you today?

folding instructions

STEP 1: Express yourself on a piece of paper—as you may have read, Bob used a six-by-nine writing pad. It's okay to use other sizes, though; just make sure it's not a square page for this type of folding. You'll want something that is taller than it is wide, situated in portrait style (as opposed to landscape).

STEP 2: (a) Fold the note in half from the top down—horizontally. **(b)** Then fold it in half again. Your page will now look like a short rectangle (much wider than it is tall).

STEP 3: Now you're in full origami mode. Starting at the top left corner of the rectangle, fold the corner down to the bottom of your rectangle (the opposite edge of the paper). There will now be a point at the left end of your paper. Take that point and fold directly across (like you're mirroring that triangle to the other side). The paper will now look like a less-wide rectangle.

Folding Instructions

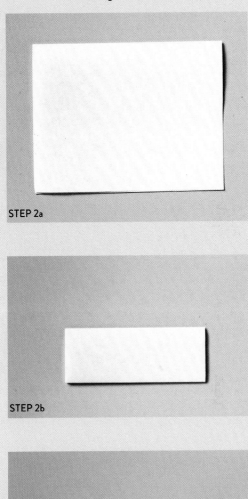

STEP 2a

STEP 2b

STEP 3

STEP 4: Take the bottom left corner (which is now bursting with triangles) and fold it upward. You'll now have a point at the top right of your paper. Take a breather.

STEP 5: You are now looking at a shape that cannot be folded into another complete triangle—so this is where you start to come to a close. Look at the right edge of your rectangle and notice that this side will be folded "into" the pocket of the triangle you have made. To do this, you'll take the top right corner and fold it down to meet the edge of the triangle. And then take the bottom right corner and fold it up to meet the other edge of the triangle.

STEP 6: If you press down on the top right edge of the triangle shape you previously created, you'll notice the pocket that has been made in your triangle. Fold the smaller triangle on your right side into that pocket.

Cut out the final page of this book to make your own folded note for a loved one!

Folding Instructions

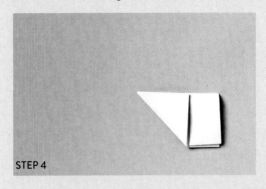

STEP 4

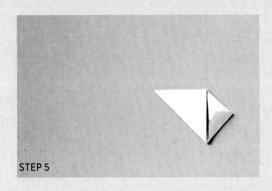

STEP 5

STEP 6

MICHAEL SINGER

JOANNA GUEST is a proud daughter who enjoys talking loudly and often about her family. She left a career in politics to focus on *Folded Wisdom*. She holds a bachelor's degree in Family Studies and Human Development from the University of Arizona and a master's of Public Policy from Georgetown University.

Folded Wisdom is her first book and she looks forward to someday plagiarizing her dad's sentiments to her own children.